THE ARCHITECT'S POCKET GUIDE TO PORTFOLIO DESIGN

This is an essential guide for architecture and design students as well as current professionals struggling to put together an effective portfolio.

There is too often a haphazard approach to architecture portfolio design and creation. Without a fundamental understanding of basic graphic design principles, portfolios can seem garish and disjointed, doing a disservice to the work on show and the designers' professional potential. This concise and highly visual guide explains the fundamental principles of portfolio creation, provides dos and don'ts, common mistakes, and analysis of a diverse range of both successful and unsuccessful samples. Aspirational, innovative design work is also presented alongside detailed commentary breaking down the reasons why it works. Chapters step through the complete process in an intuitive way, covering purpose, curation, form, layout, content and review, while providing both digital and print techniques.

Following the framework laid out in this book will quickly and effectively elevate any architecture portfolio, allowing you to showcase your work in the most professional way possible.

Zuzana Kubišová teaches in the College of Architecture & Environmental Design at Kent State University and works at J. KURTZ Architects in Cleveland, Ohio.

T0372206

Designed cover image by Zuzana Kubišová.

First published 2025
by Routledge
4 Park Square, Milton Park, Abingdon, Oxon OX14 4RN

and by Routledge
605 Third Avenue, New York, NY 10158

*Routledge is an imprint of the Taylor & Francis Group,
an informa business*

British Library Cataloguing-in-Publication Data
A catalogue record for this book is available from the British Library

Library of Congress Cataloging-in-Publication Data
Names: Kubišová, Zuzana, author.
Title: The architect's pocket guide to portfolio design / Zuzana Kubišová.
Description: Abingdon, Oxon : Routledge, 2025. | Includes index. |
Identifiers: LCCN 2024014234 | ISBN 9781032704883 (hardback) | ISBN
9781032704838 (paperback) | ISBN 9781032704913 (ebook)
Subjects: LCSH: Architecture portfolios--Design.
Classification: LCC NA1996 .K83 2025 | DDC 650.14/2--dc23/eng/20240620
LC record available at https://lccn.loc.gov/2024014234

ISBN: 978-1-032-70488-3 (hbk)
ISBN: 978-1-032-70483-8 (pbk)
ISBN: 978-1-032-70491-3 (ebk)

DOI: 10.4324/9781032704913

Publisher's Note
This book has been prepared from camera-ready copy
provided by the author.

THE ARCHITECT'S POCKET GUIDE TO PORTFOLIO DESIGN

Zuzana Kubišová

Routledge
Taylor & Francis Group

LONDON AND NEW YORK

TABLE OF CONTENTS

— WHAT IS
AN ARCHITECTURE
PORTFOLIO

An architecture portfolio tells a visual story of your professional journey, and expresses your artistic vision. Through careful consideration of imagery, text, format, composition and many other design elements, you have the power to bring your ideas to life and create a work that reveals your full potential. Your portfolio is not simply a display of your architectural talents, but it demonstrates your understanding of the design process and your own design philosophy. This self-interpretation of your individuality and passion should convey your spirit. The architectural portfolio, then, becomes a manifesto of who you are and what you stand for. It is the declaration of your design beliefs.

You present an overall design, but in addition every visual image you present in your portfolio — whether render, sketch, illustration, photograph, line drawing or even textual arrangement — helps to reveal not only your design ability, but your personality and character.

DO understand, your portfolio is itself a design project.

A portfolio can take many forms and serve multiple purposes. But whether digital or physical, online or offline, academic or professional, the essence of a portfolio remains the same: it is the first impression you give a prospective employer, client or academic institution. In most cases, someone's encounter with your portfolio is your chance at the possibility of acceptance. A chance — perhaps one chance — at opportunity and success. A well-crafted portfolio opens doors for you, to scholarships or advanced study, to first employment or to expanded professional opportunities. To a career! Your portfolio can have a terrific impact on your life!

STEP 1

IDENTIFYING

RESEARCHING

PORTFOLIO MEDIUMS

COMMON MISTAKES

— START
IDENTIFY PURPOSE

The first Step is to understand the fundamental purpose behind creating your portfolio. You must understand what your essential options are before you can choose. You want to get started, of course, but you have to prepare to get started. To prepare a thoughtful path and a well-made portfolio, this Step presents your first choices and the issues with each of them. Foremost, you want to tailor your portfolio to best align with your audience. But, who is your intended audience?

— IDENTIFYING

WHO ARE YOU

Before you even begin to define your audience, it is critical not to skip past what may seem obvious: know yourself. Take a moment to identify your goals and your values. By understanding what drives you and what you're most passionate about, and allowing this to radiate through your portfolio, you will implicitly say who you are. That clear articulation of yourself should inform all decisions from start to finish throughout your portfolio. How you declare yourself could make all the difference in getting your foot in the door.

WHO ARE YOU CREATING THIS FOR

DO tailor portfolios to specific audiences.

Beyond knowing yourself, the next most important knowledge is who you are trying to talk to. In general terms, you might already have an audience in mind for your portfolio, or you may have deliberately chosen to remain open to various possibilities, creating a more general and adaptable portfolio. Regardless of whether you are certain about your aims, you need to begin establishing a clear set of well-informed perceptions about who your target audience will be and then aim to appeal to their unique perspectives and special interests.

WHAT ARE THE MAIN PORTFOLIO CATEGORIES

The key to portfolio design strategy lies in understanding the differences in portfolio forms and purposes tailored for diverse occasions at various stages of your career. Your portfolio will have different aims, whether you are a student applying for graduate school, submitting a portfolio review or scholarship application, seeking internships, participating in competitions, applying for positions in academia or professional firms, or preparing for client meetings. Each of these situations comes with specific requirements and opportunities. To navigate these varied circumstances, be prepared to create different portfolios or adjust a single one to cater to different audiences. Generally, however, portfolios can be broadly classified into two primary categories:

- **academic**
- **professional**

WHAT IS AN ACADEMIC PORTFOLIO

An academic portfolio should ideally be shorter than a professional one. The content of the academic portfolio should focus on demonstrating your potential rather than merely showcasing your accomplishments. In other words, the aim of an academic portfolio is to present how you think about architecture — not just in terms of completed structures but more as architectural concepts, design processes and research interests, all presented in a concise manner. The portfolio serves as your opportunity to showcase the depth of your intellectual engagement with the field.

DON'T hesitate to contact the program coordinator to be sure of their requirements.

4

WHAT IS A PROFESSIONAL PORTFOLIO

The professional portfolio, in contrast, should primarily focus on presenting architectural design projects and professional practice. Considering that reviewers in the professional world are more likely to have limited time, your goal is to stand out and leave a strong impression on prospective employers or clients. So, it is paramount that you highlight key projects that showcase not only the aesthetic appeal of your designs but also demonstrate your technical prowess and full grasp of the process and rigor of the profession. The portfolio is your platform to prove that you are not just a designer but a problem solver and a strategic thinker.

— RESEARCHING

WHAT TO LEARN ABOUT AUDIENCE

DO the research! A few hours of research about the specific audience may prevent disappointment.

Even though with both categories of portfolios you aim to display your best work, they are never the same document. Beyond that, different institutions or firms will have their own distinct interests and purposes and may have specific criteria or provide particular directions. Graduate programs and prospective employers will each look for distinct qualities in successful applicants. This is why thorough research is a critical step before you even begin to compose your portfolio. Only then can you begin to strategize on how to effectively communicate with your audience and shape your portfolio accordingly. Know your audience!

When applying for an academic program, you need to first carefully examine the materials that the school provides. This involves a careful review of their websites to comprehend the

ACADEMIC PORTFOLIO

1__emphasis on design and theoretical explorations

2__projects that support your personal statement

3__present a variety of your work /photographs, sculptures, paintings.../ and tools used /pencils, watercolor, digital software.../

4__show the process of your work, and the way you think /sketches, diagrams etc./

5__five strong projects are enough to express your best work

PROFESSIONAL PORTFOLIO

*1__emphasis on technical skills
and work experience
2__projects that show specialized
skills and creative capacity
3__projects that support your identity
4__variety of project types
and scales to highlight your
range and capabilities
5__show work that reveals your
process and broad set of tools
/ digital software, pencils, modeling.../
6__six-eight strong projects
are enough to express
your best work*

program's mission, core values, and institutional requirements. Understanding the program's expectations is key to making an informed decision about whether it is the right fit for you. If it's possible, you should consider visiting the school to gain firsthand experience of the campus environment and actually talk to faculty. Additionally, making reasonable personal contacts and inquiries with the administration or faculty could provide you with special insights. Here are a few of the most basic questions you must have answers for:

DO seek advice about program from professors and current students.

- **What are the graduate program values, specialties?**
- **What are the deadlines for portfolio submission?**
- **What are the format and submission requirements?**

The same need for research applies to portfolios aimed at a professional firm. A thorough examination of the job description and required qualifications can prevent you from a potential misalignment with your audience. Therefore, dedicate enough time for reviewing the firm's website to understand their design philosophy, workflows, range of projects, and the values expressed in their completed work. Above all, be honest with yourself and assess whether working with them would bring satisfaction and if your skills would be a valuable asset to the firm. Though the opportunities may be less likely than with a school, any personal contact with the firm, even indirectly, can provide insights into their culture and needs. Here are some questions you should try to answer about professional firms:

- **What is the firm's design philosophy?**
- **What is their focus, range of projects?**
- **What are their needs?**
- **What are their requirements?**

— PORTFOLIO MEDIUMS

WHAT ARE THE MOST
COMMON PORTFOLIO MEDIUMS

Effective messaging always requires alignment with the audience. However, the medium that carries your message can allow for great adaptability and versatility, and can be multi-faceted. As the diversity of architectural practices and academic institutions increases, you need to first understand the specific portfolio forms that each audience requires. The three most common portfolio forms are defined by the media through which they are presented:

physical portfolio •
digital portfolio •
online portfolio •

There is no simple right or wrong answer as to whether to decide on a physical or digital portfolio. Depending on the audience, your choice might be already predetermined. But perhaps you have the opportunity to choose for yourself and want to have printed and digital forms since today, having both of the mediums is nearly a necessity. Especially when it comes to an academic application, the digital portfolio may be required, but if you are applying to a professional firm, you may benefit from having a physical portfolio for an in-person interview to give a sense of the full quality, determination, and experience of your work. The truth is, there is really no reason not to have multiple versions of your portfolio. Step 3, though, will give the full details of each portfolio form, which will help you to navigate your decisions.

PHYSICAL PORTFOLIO

why you should create
a physical portfolio

full control over it

demonstrates effort

no file size limit

pleasing tactile experience

no distractions from tech issues

what to expect when
making a physical
portfolio

can be expensive

difficult to share

complicated to update and refine

costly to reproduce and distribute

DIGITAL PORTFOLIO

*why you should create
a digital portfolio*

*easy to update and customize
ability to share videos and audio files
allows interactivity
easily published online
ability to zoom in*

*what the limitations
are of a digital
portfolio*

*poor visibility on smaller screens
limited by file size
loss of physicality and uniqueness
dependent on technology*

WHAT ARE THE COMMON
PORTFOLIO TYPES

Be aware that across the common media forms, there are essentially three broad types of portfolios in both academic and professional scenarios:

- **sample portfolio**
- **full portfolio**
- **leave-behind**

WHAT IS A SAMPLE
PORTFOLIO

The sample portfolio serves as a concise and practical version of your full portfolio. The primary purpose of a sample portfolio is to pique the interest of your audience and create a positive impression, often before an interview. Although sample portfolios are mainly used for professional audiences, they can be valuable or even required in academic situations. This heavily curated version allows you to highlight your most representative and relevant work, giving your audience a clear idea of your expertise and your character. As the emphasis in a sample portfolio is on quality over quantity, focus on highlighting a few key projects in detail, accompanied by concise descriptions, and impactful visuals. To keep it succinct and to the point, aim for 5–15 pages, including a bio summary and resume.

DON'T jam your sample portfolio with too many images. Usually two images per page are enough.

WHAT IS A FULL
PORTFOLIO

A full portfolio, on the other hand, should be a much more comprehensive presentation and is still commonly used as the first introduction via submission or email. In a professional environment, however, it is not uncommon to present this full version of your portfolio after an initial interest has been shown in response to the sample portfolio. The full portfolio gives you an opportunity to expand on a number of presented projects and allows you to document them with more extensive narratives and complete sets of drawings and visuals.

Even though a full portfolio does allow you to elaborate, keep in mind that brevity has value in a busy world. Your portfolio need not include every project you've completed. Strive to achieve a balance between showcasing your projects and not overwhelming your audience. Therefore, for a professional audience, it's best to stay within 50 pages as a more extensive document may lose the audience's attention or even give the impression of being inadequately curated. In academia, especially, the true measure of success lies not in the number of projects, but rather in their depth, intellectual rigor, and research endeavor. A concise, impactful presentation formatted to 20–25 pages should send a clear and confident message that still effectively highlights your accomplishments.

DO highlight award-winning or completed projects, if you have any. It emphasizes your success.

If you are a student entering the profession for the first time, your full portfolio should feature a diverse selection of all the projects that have shaped your architectural perspective and illustrate your range as a designer. In other words, showcase not only visually striking designs but also any specialized skills acquired during your studies, such as 3D modeling, rendering, or proficiency in specific software relevant to the job. For an early professional /1–3 years experience/, make sure to include various projects at different stages of development, unveiling your enhanced design and technical abilities. Presenting one or two pieces of your student work can also be beneficial, as employers are still interested in your foundation. As you advance in your career /3–8 years of experience/, the full portfolio should reflect your well-rounded knowledge and experience in the field. This means focusing on presenting your best work while maintaining diversity.

WHAT IS A
LEAVE-BEHIND

Following an interview meeting, it can be a thoughtful gesture to provide a "leave-behind." A leave-behind is typically a single printed piece that features a single project or theme from your portfolio. The goal of a leave-behind is to prolong your presence after the meeting, serving as a gentle reminder of the potential you bring to the table. Leave-behinds can take various forms, including business cards, thank-you postcards, self-promotional flayers, or even small posters. Despite the name, a leave-behind can sometimes be sent ahead, before an interview meeting and act as a preview of your core skills and attentive interest.

WHY IS FLEXIBILITY
IMPORTANT

These various portfolio forms and types often overlap and should not be mutually exclusive. Creating a portfolio is not a one-time choice. In fact you may end up using each of these forms and types, and so adapting a flexible approach might be your most important strategy.

DO keep previous versions of your portfolios. It'll save you a lot of time.

The importance of flexibility will become evident as you will most likely need to develop diverse portfolios to accommodate different audiences. Also, as you progress in your profession, you will need to incorporate new work and refine project selections to present evolving skills. Both of these scenarios will require serious effort and time to adjust your portfolio. Unless you want to create an entirely new version each time, embracing flexibility and adaptability will make your core portfolio remain useful over the years.

DO make your portfolio easily customizable so that it can speak to different audiences.

Ensuring consistency in the portfolio layout will guarantee flexibility, allowing you to accommodate diverse content types while maintaining a cohesive overall design. This is readily achieved by leveraging a modular grid system, enabling the smooth addition, removal, or resizing of content. You'll find a detailed discussion of modular grids in Step 5.

— COMMON MISTAKES

UNREALISTIC TIMELINE

DO remember that creative work requires concentration.

Assembling a quality portfolio often requires more time than you initially anticipate, possibly even two or three times longer. Assuming that you can complete a good portfolio overnight is unrealistic and can result in a poor collection of work that suggests wishful thinking and poor time management. So be honest with yourself and establish some appropriate times within a realistic schedule. While much depends on your deadline, generally you should give yourself at least a 2–3-hour window when you work. This allows you to fully focus whenever you are actually laying out your portfolio. Creative work needs concentration. When your time is limited, realistically recognizing your available time will help you, at the very least, to work effectively with a looming deadline.

MISALIGNMENT WITH YOUR AUDIENCE IS WASTEFUL

It is imperative to carefully read the requirements and expectations when working on a portfolio. In both cases, professional or academic, neglecting to align the portfolio projects with the target audience's demands can limit your immediate opportunities and waste your resources. If you are a professional, you must go through the job description closely, paying attention to the software requirements, personal qualities, experience and qualifications. For academic portfolios, it is crucial to align your portfolio projects with the program's interests and particular specialties.

STEP 2

ORGANIZING

CURATING

PACING

COMMON MISTAKES

— CURATION
GATHER AND EDIT

After you clarify your purpose, the next step is to gather your work. This process may seem overwhelming, particularly if your files lack systematic organization. This Step will, therefore, first focus on establishing an effective organizational system, one that will facilitate the current portfolio process and also pay off with effortless future referencing. The main aim of this Step, however, is to guide you in the curation process: how to plan out and strategically select your work.

— ORGANIZING

DO organize your files! You will save time, energy and a lot of frustration.

To ensure a smooth and efficient portfolio creation process, you need to dedicate some time to organizing your files into meaningful categories for easy and quick access. This process should include adequate labeling of your digital files. Often, though, this organization process is neglected and put off to some never-arriving moment when "I'll have time to organize." But actually, it is a time-saving practice that pays off right now in the portfolio process as you thoroughly evaluate and curate your work. And down the line, you will greatly benefit from the organizational effort as it'll be easier to locate specific files or track progress. If you haven't implemented this strategy, now is an ideal time to establish it in your workflow. While there are many ways to organize your work, the most effective way is to think in generic categories such as:

by chronology – dates, weeks,... •
by types – plans, visualizations, research,... •
by medium – Rhino, Revit, Photoshop, 3d Max,... •

As you go through the categorization process, it's possible you'll come across forgotten projects that may have the potential to be a part of your portfolio. At the same time, it's also possible that there are some projects with no value. This presents an opportunity to eliminate irrelevant files and archive others. Clearing the clutter will ultimately make it easier to manage the works with definite or potential value.

WHY USE
A LABEL SYSTEM

Effective file organization is not just about arranging files in a systematic manner but also about assigning clear and descriptive names to them. This may seem like a small step, but it can save you a lot of time and effort in the long run, as it allows you to quickly recognize the contents of a file without having to open it first. Such a label can look like "DublinHall ExteriorRenderingWithEffects" or "MiamiMall_ElevationB_ LineDrawing." A recommended practice is to start the label with a date and then continue with naming the specific outputs and their details, such as the "2024.10.17_Miami Mall. ElevationB.Line Drawing." This practice is particularly helpful if you have a lot of iterations of similar files.

So, next time in the midst of a hectic schedule, while it may be tempting to overlook this step, take a few extra seconds to name your files appropriately. This simple act will streamline your work.

WHY ARCHIVE
WORK FILES

Archiving your work on a regular basis is absolutely critical. As a student, you should archive your work at least once every semester after your final review. As a professional, it's good practice to archive your work every six months. Archiving involves a level of curation. You don't need to keep every

DO get used to backing up your files. It's going to save you time and a headache.

last file, but you want to hold on to every file you might need. However, in addition to archiving, you should also back up your files, which should be done repetitively but without worrying about curation. This precautionary measure of always maintaining a copy of your work will prevent you from completely losing your files in case of any unexpected technical issues.

HOW TO PROPERLY PHOTOGRAPH WORK

Good organization also requires a good recording of your work. Physical models can be difficult to manage and store over time, but establishing and maintaining a good photographic record of your creations will always pay off.

When it comes to model photography, you want to match the excellence of the work itself with professionally executed photography. Therefore, to achieve high-quality photographs of your architecture models, you need to ensure that you have the right equipment, such as:

a good camera •
good lighting •
plain, solid backdrops •

DO consider back-lighting your model to create a dramatic effect.

Good cameras with a high resolution are more easily accessed these days, but don't take your camera work for granted. Additional accessories or techniques, such as a tripod or a steady surface, may help you avoid blurring the images. Likewise, if working with a professional camera, using a remote trigger can further minimize camera shake. Adequate lighting also shouldn't be taken lightly, especially when it comes to highlighting the details and the textures of your model. To achieve quality lighting, it's best to work with two light sources. The first one should be a direct light, which points straight at the model and creates shadows. The second

FILE ORGANIZATION EXAMPLES

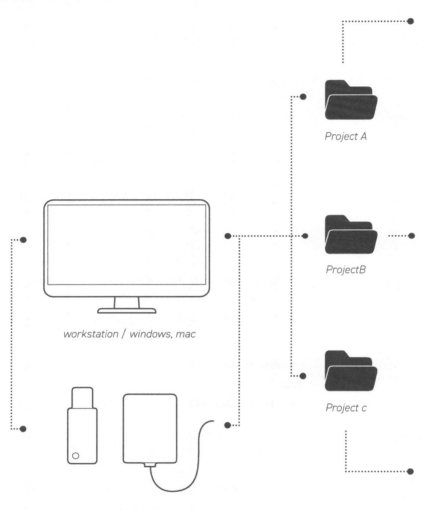

workstation / windows, mac

Project A

ProjectB

Project c

backup / UBS, HDD

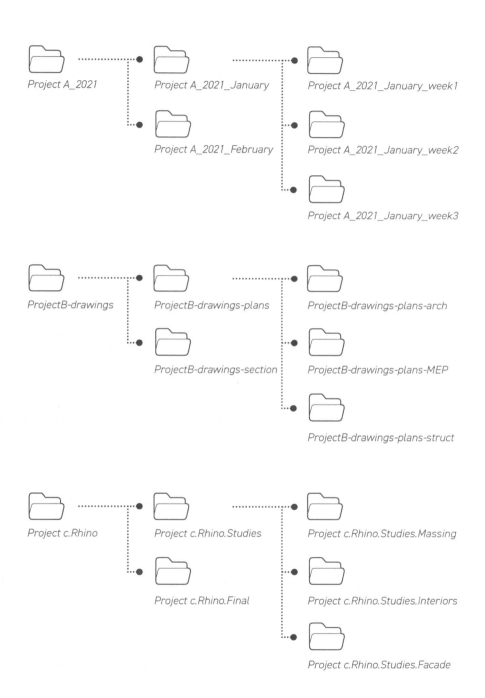

one is indirect light, which should diffuse the shadows. This light can be reflected off a wall or, the best option if available, an umbrella. Alternatively, you can also use a diffuse light — as filtered by translucent fabric, for instance — that will create soft, natural-looking light. The backdrop should be a neutral color sheet or a surface of solid color that doesn't distract from the model but instead complements it. If you are fortunate enough to have access to photography studios at your school or firm, it is definitely worth considering using them. If you are new to model photography, it's best to reach out to experienced professionals with technical and compositional experience to help elevate the quality of your photos.

DO include recognizable objects in the photo to convey the scale of the model.

When photographing your models, keep in mind that plain or mundane views without a clear purpose provide no message. Instead, make sure that the views you take help the audience understand your intentions and the main ideas of your project. Experiment with different perspectives, focuses and framing, as well as angles, such as eye level, overhead and close-ups. Keep experimenting until you achieve a holistic view of your model with all the richness and essence of your design, including the model's intricate details and tactile qualities. Finally, remember that your model may be beautifully designed and constructed, but the photograph still needs to capture its quality and meaning. If your photographs don't do justice to your model, it may be necessary to refine your model or to develop your photography technique more fully.

DO back away from the model when taking elevation views to prevent keystone distortion.

After you capture your images, it's worth considering post-processing to enhance the photographic quality and bring out the image's full potential. Image editing software such as Adobe Photoshop, Lightroom, or GIMP can help take your photos to another level by utilizing simple tools such as contrast, saturation, brightness, and sharpening. Post-processing is also essential for removing any unwanted defects like disruptive background elements or dust spots that may have been present in the original image. Additionally, keystone distortions, which are simple perspective anomalies created by the angle of your viewpoint, can be easily corrected with an image transformation tool available in image editing software.

HOW TO DO OUTDOOR
PHOTOGRAPHY

DO pay attention to the weather forecast to plan out photographing outside.

Photographing a physical model outside is also possible and sometimes unavoidable, particularly if you have an outdoor installation. Shooting outside comes with various challenges and considerations that are different from an indoor setup, but you can leverage these potential problems to your advantage. For example, the unpredictability of the most significant factor, natural light, is often considered a disadvantage. However, by paying extra attention to the direction and quality of light throughout the day, you may be able to discover unique lighting atmospheres that add an authentic touch to your photographs. If you do not have the luxury of time, taking photos during the golden hour /early morning or late afternoon/ is often a favorable option, as the light is soft and warm. Alternatively, you can take photos on a cloudy day when the light is more diffuse. Be mindful of harsh shadows caused by direct sunlight /especially midday/, which can affect the visibility of details on your physical model.

Outdoor photography also depends a lot on the background and composition. While you may have limited options, it's best to keep the background to a minimum to avoid visual distraction, which will make photo editing easier. The background you choose should complement your model without overpowering it. Similarly, a sufficient contrast between your model and the background is necessary for the model to stand out. Make sure to capture your model from a variety of angles to provide different perspectives and options for the background. If you are shooting outdoor installations, use objects or figures in the foreground and background to add depth, scale, and interest to your composition. However, be careful with unrelated objects that are not on the same scale as your model, as it can create a visual discord. In such cases, either remove the object /manually or later by photo editing/ or match your model to the scale of the object with an appropriate distance.

CURATING —

HOW TO SELECT
OBJECTIVELY

Once you have done the work of organizing your projects and understand what you have available, you can begin the preliminary selection process. The biggest challenge you may encounter as you start your selection and, in fact, through the whole development of your portfolio, is to objectively evaluate your strengths and qualities. This challenge requires you to take a step back from your own design work and look at it as objectively as possible. Inviting other eyes, such as classmates or coworkers, can provide valuable feedback and fresh perspectives, helping you better understand how others perceive your work. Don't hesitate to ask for input during the preliminary selection as well as during the more focused curation process.

DON'T treat your portfolio as a catalog of your work history.

WHAT ARE
THE SELECTION AIMS

The first and foremost consideration in selecting your work should be to prioritize quality over quantity. This means being conscientious and critical and only including projects that truly showcase your strengths and the breadth of your skills. A good starting point is to choose projects that have received recognition for their quality, such as those with higher grades, competition wins, or positive feedback from clients or colleagues. However, as you gain more experience through professional experience or studies, you'll better understand your strengths and may consider including projects that may not have been ultimately successful but in which you recognize quality and potential.

DON'T include similar projects. Instead, choose ones that expand the portrait of you.

When curating images for your projects, remember that the images you choose should convey diverse and unique information. Even if multiple images are equally compelling, prioritize those that best showcase your potential or tell the viewer something different or new. Including multiple images showcasing the same or similar information may increase the number of your best sure-fire images but could also reduce the attention given to more unique works. If you just stay with what's obviously best for you, some valuable images that could enhance and better communicate your project or even your identity may get squeezed out of your final curation, especially since your portfolio length is often constrained. Therefore, you must be strategic in the selection process to ensure your project conveys a full range of the best material within the limits of your space.

DO keep in mind that image diversity shows depth.

HOW TO BEGIN WITH PRELIMINARY SELECTION

DO remember that three great images are better than seven good ones.

Curating can be an overwhelming and time-consuming process. However, there's a way to make this decision-making process more manageable — by categorizing your work into three groups: YES, NO, and MAYBE. This project grouping method should help you to evaluate each project or image on its own merits and assign the appropriate label based on project quality, clarity and visual appeal. As you are categorizing all of your work into these three main groups, try to keep these five questions in mind:

- Is the work complete, thoroughly done?
- Does the project exhibit clarity?
- Do I have a variety of project typologies?
- How much reworking will a lesser project need?
- Is the work distinct, part of my identity?

WHICH PROJECTS TO PUT
INTO THE YES CATEGORY

Generally, the group "YES" should feature all the work that strongly presents your skills, technical and creative processes, and design ideas. Remember that for both audiences, academic and professional, it is essential to include a variety of projects. Generally, you want to present projects that demonstrate the following qualities:

- design potential – design projects, visual representation
- technical understanding – technical drawings, construction details
- scope of experience – projects, internships and competitions
- interests – specialized skills, academic research

Beyond selecting your strongest work, however, you need to remember your specific goals and align your curation with your target audience. For instance, if you're applying for a position in a residential firm, your focus should be on a certain typological range. Beyond showcasing a series of typological projects, your portfolio would benefit by presenting projects with distinctive and creative design features, along with an understanding of construction details. You want to help prospective employers or clients get a sense of your design style and capabilities and give them a sense of what would set you apart from others in residential design. However, if you are pursuing a graduate program, you should aim to highlight not only your exceptional design projects but also your intellectual curiosity and distinctive research interests.

DO include physical models in your curated selection to present your ideas in diverse ways.

DO select some sketches to show how you think.

Although alignment must shape your curation, don't give up on presenting a balanced portrait. Choose additional works such as art pieces, photography, graphic design, or any other examples of creative effort and rounded interests. These can serve as practical demonstrations of your abilities and contribute to telling the story of your unique identity and appeal. If you manage to compile a well-rounded portfolio, you are much more likely to communicate your abilities effectively as well as stand out in a competitive environment.

WHICH PROJECTS TO PUT INTO THE NO CATEGORY

DON'T present only collaborative projects. Instead present only one or two to show your teamwork abilities.

Category "NO" includes all work that is not relevant to the portfolio's purpose, unfinished projects, weakly executed or outdated work. Also, if you have a collaborative project where you had a minimal role with limited impact on the design or its execution, it's also best to place it into the "NO" category. Such projects ultimately reveal your weaknesses instead of highlighting your strengths. Keep in mind that it is for your own benefit to be overly critical in this evaluation process. So don't feel guilty about eliminating projects that could endanger your success or, at the very least, bring the guilt of using others' talents.

WHICH PROJECTS TO PUT INTO THE MAYBE CATEGORY

DON'T forget that early student work /that has good intentions/often needs revisions and additions.

The last category, with the label "MAYBE," comprises projects that are not absolutely essential but could still provide some value to your portfolio presentation. Perhaps the images are strong, but you are uncertain about their relevancy to your audience. The "MAYBE" collection will also include projects that may have potential but need further development or refinement to become part of your portfolio. Whether or not to include any of them in your final curated collection depends mainly on three key factors:

• your available time
• the number of such projects
• the project's diversity

If you are revisiting at least some work from this category, don't hesitate to refine some of the content of those projects in the "YES" category as well. Remember, it is a common practice to revisit work created earlier in your career, but it's always a question of prioritizing your time when you consider revising. Early work does not have to be re-imagined, but drawings and overall presentation should be brought up to your current standards. If you're short on time, always focus on quality over quantity and remove any subpar projects or images from the final curation. Even a single poor image can undermine a lot of good work and hurt your chances of securing an important opportunity.

When you do revise your work, you ought to develop a habit of preserving your original files. And so, before making any edits, always create a copy to ensure that your original work remains intact and unchanged. This way, you can feel confident experimenting with different editing techniques without worrying about losing your original work.

DO create a copy of your original image before you edit it. Always.

WHAT TO PRESENT WITHOUT AN ARCHITECTURE BACKGROUND

If you are applying for a graduate architecture program without an architectural background, you may be unsure of what to include in your portfolio. Keep in mind that your portfolio should showcase not only your visual thinking skills but also your overall thought process. So, as long as your portfolio reflects your creative potential, critical thinking, problem-solving and enthusiasm for the field, your application will be taken seriously.

DO remember that a variety of project groups shows the versatility of your skills.

While some programs require basic drawing skills and three-dimensional aptitude, others evaluate your overall potential. Either way, you shouldn't dismiss the opportunity to visually communicate your ideas in some form and should try to develop some visual representations before applying to school. Any creative project that presents your current design sensibilities can be a tremendous asset. For example, projects such as simple drawings, paintings, photography, or even pottery can bring valuable dimensions to your portfolio. If you are more technically inclined, you might want to showcase your proficiency in digital tools such as 3D modeling, graphic design, or any software that can be useful in the field of architecture. Additionally, incorporating personal projects related to architecture or design, such as home renovations, custom furniture pieces, or some interior designs, can be equally impactful. If your background is much more scientific, presenting research papers or essays related to design or relevant fields can also reveal your potential as a creative thinker. Lastly, remember that a well-written statement demonstrating your motivation in architecture can outweigh specific gaps in your skills.

The bottom line is to emphasize your individual strengths and interests and to present your work in a clear, compelling design.

— PACING

WHY PACING MATTERS

The pace at which you present your portfolio can impact how viewers engage with, comprehend, and appreciate your work. Organizing your projects in a deliberate and purposeful way that creates a rhythm will allow your audience to perceive each piece individually as well as the context and progression of your work.

There are various ways to organize your projects, each with its own advantages and disadvantages. Unless your audience requires a specific organization, you should aim for creativity and originality. A less predictable pattern can pace your content in a more engaging and captivating manner. Here are basic strategies you can start with:

- **chronological method**
- **three-act method**
- **category method**
- **relevancy method**

WHAT IS THE CHRONOLOGICAL METHOD

A chronological order is perhaps the most used method because it's straightforward and often required, especially when it comes to academic applications. Its forthright nature provides a clear and concise snapshot of the progression of your interests and skills, design ideas, and level of responsibility throughout your architectural education and professional experience. An alternative approach is to adopt reverse chronology, starting with your most recent and likely more refined project, unfolding your development backward.

DO consider fewer projects, and more pages and depth per project.

However, if you have the option, it may be worth considering another, less conventional pacing method. The typical chronological approach, being the easiest and most common, might make your portfolio appear less distinct than others. More importantly, this approach is less likely to grab the viewer's attention right from the start with your early work. Your most developed or maybe even most relevant project gets buried toward the end as interest fades away.

DO switch up the length of projects. It will enhance the rhythm of your portfolio.

*DO consider
starting with
your strongest
project to grab the
viewer's attention.*

Arranging your portfolio in a three-act or "sandwich" method involves placing a compelling project right at the beginning to make a powerful first impression, followed by strategically interspersing stronger projects within your portfolio to sustain curiosity, and finally, showcasing the most striking project at the end for a lasting resonance. The less impressive work then will act as transitions, placed between these three stages, while still maintaining a steady level of interest from your viewer. This strategy can, therefore, create a sense of rhythm and engagement, guiding the viewer through a dynamic story of your skills and accomplishments.

The success of this strategy, however, depends a lot on the quantity of your projects and especially on the quality of your work. You shouldn't implement a three-act method if you are working on a brief sample portfolio, for example, or if you have yet to develop enough presentable work. To convey your meaningful narrative, you must have a substantial amount and depth of portfolio content /at least five projects/ that can effectively engage your audience.

Under the category method, you sort your projects into simple, logical groups and present your work one group at a time. This approach inherently establishes a natural cohesion in the narrative you present.

While you have the flexibility to define your groups in various ways, some of the most apparent categories include:

PORTFOLIO PACING

chronological method

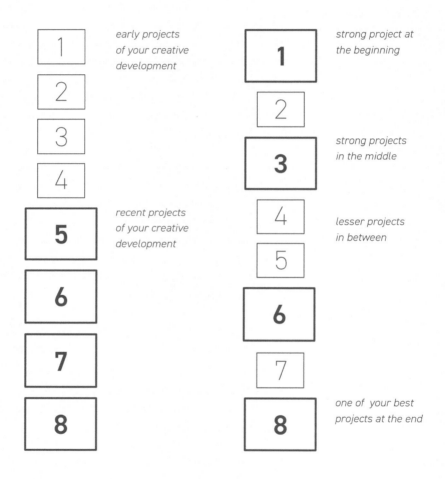

early projects
of your creative
development

recent projects
of your creative
development

strong project at
the beginning

strong projects
in the middle

lesser projects
in between

one of your best
projects at the end

three-act method

category method

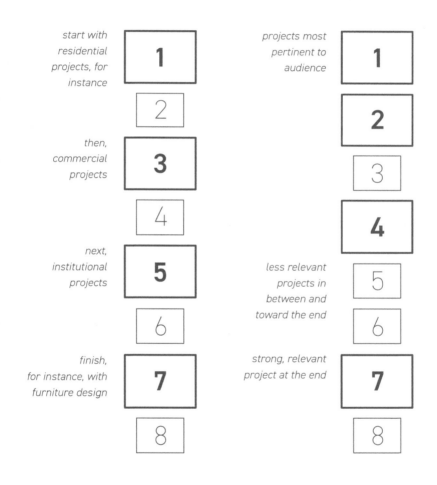

start with residential projects, for instance

1

2

then, commercial projects

3

4

next, institutional projects

5

6

finish, for instance, with furniture design

7

8

projects most pertinent to audience

1

2

3

4

less relevant projects in between and toward the end

5

6

strong, relevant project at the end

7

8

relevancy method

- by typology /residential or commercial, or more specifically multi-dwelling, retail, schools, etc./
- by design field /architecture, product design, photography/
- by experience /professional vs academic, undergraduate vs graduate/
- by intent or objective /built, unbuilt, speculative, competitions, experimental/

This method empowers you to discuss and highlight a specific category that aligns with the job requirements or the interviewer's interest. The ease of reordering categories also works to your advantage, allowing you to tailor your presentation for different audiences by prioritizing sections that are most relevant to a particular audience while keeping the others accessible as a backup.

While the approach offers flexibility, it may fall short in creating a strong initial impression since your organization of categories doesn't necessarily start with your best work. Therefore, you should give special attention to the sequence and pacing of your projects, both from one category to another and within each group. Otherwise, your most impressive work may not be highlighted and get overlooked beneath the overall organization. Also, since this method relies on having diverse sets of projects to be able to create categories, it may not be a feasible strategy if your work lacks the necessary diversity.

DO name your categories distinctively to prevent any organizational ambiguity.

WHAT IS THE RELEVANCY METHOD

The relevancy method places a primary focus on the audience's perspective. It organizes your work based on how important and relevant each project would be to your audience. To implement this approach and to make an immediate connection with your audience, you begin by emphasizing projects that best align with their needs. Then, you move on to projects that more fully demonstrate your skill set and professional identity. Whether demonstrating problem-solving abilities, technical proficiency, or design thinking skills, your aim is to guide the audience through your experience in a way that resonates with their interests and priorities. Finally, conclude your portfolio strongly by choosing a last project that encourages discussion of their primary interests.

DO consider starting your portfolio with a built work, if you have any.

The engagement and focus that come with the relevancy method make a strong case for this being your best choice. However, if you don't have a clear understanding of your audience's interests and needs, this approach might not be effective. Similarly, its effectiveness diminishes if you lack enough projects that directly resonate with the audience. Lastly, if you are looking for a flexible approach, this method may not be the most suitable as it requires reordering your projects for each new audience.

— COMMON MISTAKES

POOR
CURATION

A comprehensive overview of your projects should be your prime concern when creating a portfolio. But that doesn't mean that you need to include every single image of your project, which often leads to an overloaded layout /see common mistakes 1/. In such instances, viewers are likely to struggle to recognize your best work amongst all the clutter and move to the next page as they get overwhelmed with too much information. You should be profoundly selective when curating. Make every single image count!

A weak curation is especially evident when it comes to presenting redundant or similar images /see common mistakes 2/. Since these images don't add any additional value and take up valuable space, which dilutes the strength of your presentation, you need to do your curation judiciously. Each image should serve a purpose in demonstrating different aspects of your project.

POOR PHOTOGRAPHY

Regardless of how impressive your model may be, poor-quality photographs can quickly diminish its quality and take away from its overall visual appeal. This is especially likely to happen when rushing through the process of photographing models, particularly when recording for future reference without a specific purpose. This haste often results in images that are blurry, less detailed, or captured from uninteresting angles, failing to highlight the uniqueness of your model /see common mistakes 3 and 4/. Taking time to experiment with different angles and positions can help you find the best visual and informative essence of your model that can fulfill multiple purposes.

DO use a backdrop or set up a neutral surface to isolate the model.

Similarly, neglecting a proper setup can fail to do justice to your model. Scenarios such as taking photographs in cluttered rooms with poor lighting can distract viewers from your work and obscure important moments of your model /see common mistakes 5/. Therefore, make sure to create a neutral, clean, and well-lit setup. It can elevate your model tremendously.

*DON'T forget to
ask for permission
to use projects
that were created
in an office.*

Always give proper credit to all the contributors while presenting collaborative work. Otherwise, it can badly impact your professional image. Although showcasing a project you collaborated on underscores your ability to work within a team, you should clearly outline your project responsibilities and contributions in a specific way and then give proper credit to everyone involved. Your prospective employers or academic committees can then better understand your abilities — as well as recognize your integrity.

CARELESS
ATTENTION

*DO acknowledge
your weaknesses.
It's part of
recognizing your
strengths and
selecting projects
strategically.*

The quality of a portfolio is a direct reflection of the effort and dedication invested in the work. If your portfolio lacks effort and finesse, it could reveal unprofessionalism and carelessness. This usually comes about through failure to revisit and refine your projects, resulting in an unfinished, unpolished, or even incomplete portfolio. The impression of carelessness may also stem from a lack of thoughtful presentation of your work, which might indicate that you haven't taken the time to select your best pieces. Investing time in selecting and refining your work with care will reflect your commitment to good work and attention to detail — qualities that are highly valued in professional and academic settings.

COMMON MISTAKES

poor curation

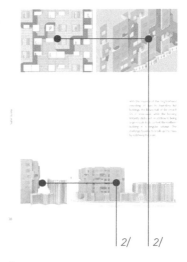

1/

2/   2/

*1/ Including too many images
can dilute the impact of otherwise
strong works.*

*2/ Including images that resemble
each other or don't have any
additional value can bore and
disengage the audience.*

*Well-done curation is not about
the amount of your content but
its quality. Therefore, be strategic
and include only those images that
reflect the variety of your skills
and, most importantly, offer new
information.*

IMAGES THIS PAGE BY LUCAS DENMEADE

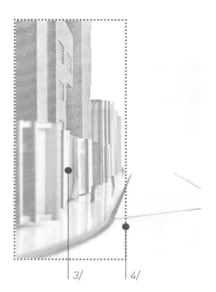

photographs

3/   4/   5/

3/ Low resolution hinders a model's visual appeal.

4/ A poor angle may lack depth and obscure a model's spatial relationships.

5/ Inappropriate background with poor lighting can diminish the perceived quality of your work.

Photograph your model from angles that reveal its best qualities. Use a simple background to keep the focus on the model itself. Optimize camera settings for high resolution.

IMAGES THIS PAGE BY LUCAS DENMEADE

STEP 3

— FORM
BASIC CHOICES

Once you have done your initial planning and have selected your work, it's time to start thinking about how you want your portfolio to look. This Step will go over the broad presentation choices available to you and what to keep in mind while deciding the overall form of your portfolio.

— SELECTING A MEDIUM

WHERE TO START
WITH THE BASIC CHOICES

At this point in the process, you should have already identified your target audience and thoughtfully curated a collection of your work. Maybe you even have a general sense of how you want your presentation to flow. Now, you can move forward to some other important choices. First, you need to determine whether to use a physical or digital medium for your portfolio. Then, you decide on the format, proportion, and page orientation. Or perhaps you just want to create a portfolio as a website. Even if the demands of your intended audience already predetermine most of these decisions, or if you already have a clear sense of how you want your portfolio to look, you should still take time to go through and understand the choices presented in this Step. That way, you can be aware of all the options available within each medium, and you can be sure to understand the constraints and potentials that will shape upcoming design choices.

HOW TO CHOOSE
A MEDIUM

Before diving into the specifics of each medium, keep in mind that in today's increasingly digitalized world, having a strong digital portfolio at the early stages of the recruitment process is a baseline. Whether it's for professional or academic purposes, the majority of requests will likely involve sending or uploading a digital version, even if you have your own website. While the need for a physical portfolio has become much more optional, it still holds strong value. This becomes evident, especially during the interview process where tangible material makes for effective communication. Regardless of your choice, be aware that each medium comes with a variety of options, challenges and distinctions that may impact your design decisions. The following sections will address and evaluate the pros and cons of all your choices.

PHYSICAL PORTFOLIO —

WHAT ARE THE BENEFITS
OF A PHYSICAL PORTFOLIO

Physical portfolios have distinctive qualities. The tactile experience of a physical portfolio can highlight the quality and detail of images in a way that screens simply cannot. In an interview, for instance, a physical portfolio can facilitate communication between you and your potential employer or client, as the act of physically presenting and discussing the contents of your portfolio can help you articulate and contextualize your work, making the interview much smoother. Such interaction may be challenging to replicate with a digital portfolio.

Compared to devices like iPads and computer monitors, a physical portfolio creates a more tangible and memorable

DON'T underestimate the power of tactile experience. It has a real impact.

42

DO remember that a well-crafted physical portfolio will show off your determination.

experience. Your hands working along with your eyes create a stronger memory. Unlike simply swiping through images displayed on a screen, the physical aspect of the paper also encourages the viewer to go through every single page, thus immersing the viewer in your work and suggesting a slower pace and fuller experience. Moreover, with a physical portfolio, you establish a much more distinctive identity outside of a viewer's constant and repetitive screen time, and therefore, you have a much higher chance to separate yourself from the competition.

In the broad view, the overarching benefit of a physical portfolio is that you have full control over how the viewer sees your work — precisely as you have designed and executed it. This inherent strength of physical portfolios contrasts digital portfolios, which, despite your best designs, might end up displaying differently on various screen qualities and sizes. Additionally, don't overlook another benefit of a physical portfolio. In order to format and lay it out for printing, you essentially first create a digital portfolio. From that, you can easily create a shareable digital portfolio. It's a versatile advantage that creating a physical portfolio requires creating a digital one.

WHAT ARE THE DRAWBACKS OF A PHYSICAL PORTFOLIO

Naturally, however, a physical portfolio also has drawbacks. Physical production can be a substantial investment of both money and time, especially when you need to update and tailor your portfolio to various audiences. Costs associated with print tests, final prints, paper, cover and binding all need to be taken into account when working on a physical portfolio. Additionally, making tweaks and adjustments to get it "just right" can be more challenging with physical production as opposed to the flexibility offered by digital media.

The physical portfolio takes time. A desirable presentation for your portfolio will require patience and careful layout, but the process of physical production — color-checking, printing, reprinting, binding — presents its own set of time-consuming challenges that are often slow to resolve. Moreover, errors in the final product can be difficult to fix. Yet, the tangible sense of production and finality contributes to the innate quality of a physical portfolio. If time is your constraint, however, it may be best to avoid creating a physical portfolio. While a well-crafted portfolio can really impress, a poorly executed one can actually work against you.

DO stick to the standard printed sizes to avoid inefficiency and high cost.

HOW YOUR PRINT PRODUCTION MAY LIMIT YOUR CHOICES

A lot of important decisions will revolve around the early pivotal choices you make about your printing method, such as the printer type /inkjet, color laser/, printing service /professional or self-printing/ and binding options. As you make your decisions, be aware that the size of the paper you select will profoundly impact the overall appearance of your portfolio, potentially shaping and even limiting the visual style you hope to achieve. /Later in this Step, paper sizes and formats are discussed./ Below are some considerations that may help you to assess your printing and binding choices.

WHAT TO KNOW ABOUT PRINTING METHODS

Printing with both inkjet and color laser printers is affordable and readily available today. However, when deciding which one to use, you should consider the quality of color output and printing speed of the printers, both of which impact portfolio production. Inkjet printing can produce stunning, high-resolution color output, resulting in a more visually appealing final product. However, the inkjet printing process can be slow, particularly when handling large files with high-resolution images, making it a potentially time-consuming endeavor. On the other hand, color laser printing is relatively fast, though it may not provide the same level of color quality and image clarity as inkjet prints. Ultimately, the output of specific printers should be reviewed with your own eyes so you find the quality that aligns with your needs.

WHAT TO KNOW ABOUT PRINTING SERVICES

DO consider a print service. It will save you a lot of effort, time and most likely money as well.

Despite the quality of home printers available today, you may still need to use a professional print service. In the short run, this could be your least expensive and most effective option. With a professional print service, you have access to a broader range of paper types and sizes, consistent print quality and accuracy, various printing techniques and especially professional advice and guidance on issues you may encounter during the printing process. The self-printing option becomes more worthwhile when working on, for instance, a concise sample portfolio of six or so pages, or even better, a leave-behind of a single page.

WHAT TO KNOW ABOUT BINDING

Binding plays a critical role in constructing and designing a physical portfolio. The binding you choose will greatly affect the overall look and feel of your portfolio presentation, so don't take this decision lightly. What follows is a review of the commonly used options for portfolio binding. To begin, here are some basic questions that can guide your binding selection:

Should the portfolio book lay flat when opened? •
Will the images run continuous across page spreads? •
How many pages need to be bound? •

WHAT ABOUT
LOOSE-LEAF BINDING

There is nothing inherently wrong or unprofessional about keeping your portfolio unbound. This free form allows flexible order, which could be easily rearranged to fit your audience. A loose-leaf portfolio can even appear more specialized and artistic, given that such portfolios are standard in many fine arts. A distinct advantage of a loose-leaf portfolio is the potential use of unconventional paper sizes, within reason, and even heavier weights or qualities of paper. But, of course, there is a danger of your page order being mixed as reviewers go through your work, or some pages getting misplaced and lost. And, even if your work stays intact, the actual handling of your pages requires more attention — or may be perceived as more bothersome — by your reviewers.

DO keep in mind that durability of handmade bindings may be compromised if not done properly.

If you do consider a loose-leaf portfolio, it is especially important to manage your presentation professionally to avoid any sense of sloppiness or haphazardness. That being said, a loose-leaf portfolio should be encased in a folder made of durable and high-quality materials that reflect the same level of thoughtfulness as the content inside.

WHAT ABOUT
WIRE-O BINDING

The Wire-O binding is a relatively cost-effective option that provides a refined, professional look. One of its main advantages is that it allows pages to turn effortlessly and lay flat, eliminating the need to hold them open. This makes page-to-page reviews simple and clean for your presentation. The wire size and loop diameter can vary depending on the number of pages and the paperweight. This is why you should pay close attention to selecting wires and loops that are not overly large but still facilitate easy movement of your pages.

DON'T use plastic coil binding. It looks unprofessional and is aesthetically unattractive.

While the Wire-O binding method does not prevent you from allowing images to span across the spine, the physical gap created by the wire connection will disrupt such images. If this visual obstacle is not aligned with your design intentions, you may need to consider a different binding method.

WHAT ABOUT
SOFT PERFECT BINDING

Perfect /or softcover/ binding is the method wherein pages are glued together along a spine, and then a cover gets wrapped around and glued to the solid spine of the inside pages. Without a doubt, this type of binding gives your portfolio a clean, aesthetically pleasing and professional appearance at a reasonable cost. One of the key advantages of perfect binding is that it creates a compact spine that lays flat on a surface without wire connectors or the bulge of stapled paper. Additionally, this binding allows images to span across two-page spreads.

DO consider a binding that keeps the portfolio flat when open, allowing viewers to fully see your work.

If you're planning on printing a portfolio with fewer than 30 pages, perfect binding may not be the most suitable choice. The reason is that the spine requires a substantial amount of paper for the glue to take hold and secure the pages together. Another downside to consider is that, despite its neat exterior appearance, perfect binding causes pages to not lie flat when opened, requiring more effort from your audience for hands-on browsing. Additionally, the glued binding creates an area that becomes obscured in spreads, with each page disappearing into the spine. This can pose challenges in viewing the content and even result in losing some content near the inside binding. Nevertheless, there are workarounds for this issue, and Step 5 will delve into them.

WHAT ABOUT SADDLE
STITCH BINDING

Saddle stitch, also referred to as stapled binding, stands out as one of the most cost-effective and commonly used book binding methods. This technique produces a simple, reliable, yet aesthetically pleasing appearance. The process involves stapling together a set of two-page spreads at their folded center. Because of its flexibility to accommodate a variety of paper sizes, this option offers you more choices for the size of your portfolio. Moreover, with a subtle crease at the fold, this binding technique enables images to seamlessly span across two pages. Lastly, this binding technique allows the portfolio to lie relatively flat when open, which permits every bit of content to be seen right up to the interior edge without any major distraction of connectors or curved pages at the spine.

DON'T use overly expressive binding such as ribbons, twine, bolts and other handiwork.

One of the main drawbacks of saddle stitch binding is that it becomes increasingly difficult to bind together as the number of pages increases. Typically, this binding method is well-suited for projects with a page count ranging up to about 60, although this largely depends on the paper's thickness. If you try to staple-bind thicker papers or a higher amount of pages, a mechanically folded crease becomes necessary to reduce the bulkiness of the fold. In such cases, it might be better to contact a print service.

WHAT ARE THE
COVER OPTIONS

The cover of your portfolio serves as an extension of the content within. Given that the tone of your physical portfolio cover should be influenced by your entire body of selected work, it is ill-advised to design the cover before completing the inside content. However, you should start considering what type of cover you want to use. You can choose between:

DON'T try to over-design your covers with perforations, or embossing.

- **softcover**
- **hardcover**

Softcovers are flexible covers made of heavy-weight paper such as cardstock or bristol, and they can be used with various bindings. The pages can be glued to the spine for perfect binding, folded and stapled for saddle stitch, or punched and threaded for a wire-o binding. The downside of soft covers is that they are likely to fray more quickly with the less durable cover material. On the positive side, their lightweight nature makes their use and transport easier. Also, softcovers are more affordable as their production is less complicated.

Hardcovers are bound in stiff cardboard, such as book board. Attaching a hardcover to your portfolio can be complicated and expensive, and maybe not desirable since a hardbound cover tends to be heavy and less flexible. On the other hand, a chipboard, or museum board, though not as stiff, provides sturdy shell-like protection and makes a portfolio significantly more durable and formal than one with a soft cover. However, if your portfolio needs frequent updates or if cost is a significant concern, you may want to weigh that against the advantages of a more formal cover.

WHY SELECTION OF PAPER MATTERS

DO consider using vellum or cardstock as section dividers and as design components.

When creating a physical portfolio, you should give special attention to the paper selection. Since physical portfolios are meant to be viewed up close, the type of paper you choose plays a significant role in shaping the perception of your work. Here are some of the main characteristics to consider when choosing paper:

weight – standard, cardstock, vellum •
finish – matt, semi-gloss, gloss •
color – bright white, off-white, colors •
texture – smooth, rough •

Each of these qualities can have an impact on the viewer's perception of your portfolio. To make sure you're selecting the best paper for your needs, it's a good idea to check out a swatch book at a local print service. Regardless of the paper you decide on, it should align with your budget, aesthetic preferences and, importantly, its intended use. For a portfolio, you want to have strong paper, white or nearly white, that you are certain holds your printed images vividly. Be cautious not to overwhelm your portfolio with elaborate textures, weights, or vibrant colors that might distract from the content.

DO test prints to check how paper quality and type of printer affects your work.

PORTFOLIO PRINT PROCESS —

WHY IMAGE RESOLUTION AND DIMENSION MATTER

Preparing your work for actual printing requires care and a little extra patience. Your goal here is to make your images look as good in print as they do on the screen. Many times, the impact of an image can be lost in the process from screen to page. This is because images require much fuller resolution and, consequently, more file data to look clearer and more vivid on the physical page than on a screen. Therefore, before jumping into sample prints, let alone the final prints, you need to re-examine your image files, check their resolution and dimensions, and ensure that your files are optimized for printing.

HOW TO OPTIMIZE IMAGE PRINT RESOLUTION

Printed images have the potential to carry more impact, so despite the fact that optimizing your images for print can be complex and more time-consuming, the effort can be quite gratifying. Additionally, mastering image optimization demonstrates your technical skills in balancing image quality and size — a much-needed skill in visual fields like architecture.

DO keep the resolution of your images around 300 DPI to ensure high resolution.

The bottom line is that an image optimized for print will have sufficient resolution /ideally 300 DPI/ at the width and height that you choose. Also, the image should be in a file format that best maintains its color, clarity and other qualities, while at the same time, the file data size should be made as small as possible. The image will need to be compressed if its file data size is too large for reasonable file handling and printing. Here are the basic concepts and tools that will help you optimize images for print:

image resolution •
image dimensions /width and height/ •
file formats and file data size •
compression tools •
color profile •

WHY IMAGE
RESOLUTION MATTERS

DO learn how to leverage image compression.

The quality of a printed image is primarily affected by its resolution and dimensions. Image resolution is typically measured by the number of pixels an image contains, which is visually reflected in the level of detail the image holds. This resolution value is abbreviated as PPI /pixels per inch/ or DPI /dots per inch/. While PPI is typically used for digital input that pertains to screens, DPI is the standard measurement for print, which stands for the number of ink dots per inch a printer deploys on paper. When you are preparing an image for print, you need to make sure the screen image is adjusted to at least 300 DPI at 100% of the final output dimensions. If your file data size is too large, you can reduce the resolution, but don't go below 180 DPI so as to avoid undesirable pixelation and diminished quality. However, there are other ways to reduce the file data size, such as file compression which will be discussed shortly.

WHAT ARE THE IMAGE
DIMENSIONS AND RESOLUTION

So, for satisfactory print outcomes, an image should have a resolution of 300 DPI. However, you still must consider the image dimensions. Finding the right balance between image dimensions and image resolution is the key to achieving a high-quality print. The resolution and the dimensions of an image are inversely related: increase the resolution of an image and its width and height contract; decrease the resolution, and the dimensions enlarge.

Without changing the resolution of your image you can determine the maximum print dimensions for an image by checking its pixel dimensions. Simply divide the pixel width and height by 300 to find the maximum dimensions at which you can use the image while maintaining a quality resolution of 300 DPI. For instance, if your image is 1200 pixels wide and 800 pixels high, divide 1200 by 300 and 800 by 300 to determine the maximum usable width and height of the image. This tells you the image at 300 DPI should retain its quality at dimensions of 4 x 2.67 inches or smaller. /Or converted for metric users to 10.16 x 6.78 centimeters./

Still, your image might not be optimized yet, even if it will print at 300 DPI in dimensions large enough for your needs. You should still consider your file format and also, if the data size of your file is large, use compression tools.

DON'T use native Photoshop files in InDesign or other publishing softwares, as it can increase the file size. Instead, import standard file types.

WHICH FILE
FORMATS WORK BEST

Using the right image formats can help mitigate the risk of print quality issues during production, ultimately saving you time and sparing you frustration. While there are many image file formats you can choose from, some are more appropriate for printing than others. Here are some of the file formats you should use for your images:

Joint Photographic Experts Group – JPEG •
Portable Network Graphics – PNG •
Adobe Illustrator Artwork – AI •
Portable Document Format – PDF •

DON'T use a
JPEG file format
for graphics
that contain
transparencies.

JPEG is widely used for image editing and printing due to its good quality and relatively small size. The JPEG file format balances image quality with compression, and this balance can be adjusted in most image editing software. Large image files can become unworkable, but saving an image as a JPEG file can sort and systematize the data without sacrificing much clarity or color accuracy. However, be cautious when compressing and saving JPEG files, as too much compression will result in image pixelation. It's also important to understand that JPEG isn't the best format for graphics with line drawings since it can result in blurring and fuzziness of line edges. For this same reason, images that contain some text can lose sharpness in the letters. Also, for graphics that contain areas of transparency — diagrams without a background, for instance — the image ought to be saved in the PNG format, which can support transparency.

DON'T use a JPEG
format for images
in which text is a
key component.

PNG is another file format that delivers high-quality images while still maintaining a relatively small size /though usually larger than JPEG/. One of the significant benefits of PNG is its capability to display transparent areas and high-resolution images with fuller color depths. Another asset /but also a drawback/ of PNG is that it is a lossless format, meaning it condenses image data without discarding any information, unlike the JPEG format. This lossless integrity preserves the quality of an image, which is why PNG is a good choice for presenting line drawings with clarity of resolution along line edges. However, it's important to note that using this format can result in heavier file sizes, and it's not compatible with the CMYK color profile typically used in printing, which may cause colors to appear muted. Therefore, in cases where color plays a significant role, JPEG might still be the preferable choice.

The AI file format is a vector-based format that is not suitable for photographs and other colorful images. However, since vector images are not pixel-based but rather mathematic descriptions, they can be endlessly scaled without losing sharp edges or gaining heavy, resolution-dependent file sizes. This can be very useful in presenting some line work and diagrams or even graphics with text. A drawback is that the AI format is native to Adobe Illustrator software, so it can be difficult to open and edit AI files if you don't have Illustrator. But, if the file is saved in other vector formats, such as SVG, it can still be used in other editing software. With Adobe's ongoing efforts to improve cross-software compatibility, the AI format is becoming a more practical format for wider use. What's important is that AI and other vector image files can be exported to PDF files which are used for final printing.

The PDF format is quite flexible and a highly favored format for printing purposes. This format is commonly used as the final document before printing production because it can include and maintain the integrity of your edited document's layout and fonts, as well as all the graphics. Additionally, the PDF's versatility extends to printing both pixel images and vectors, making it ideal for the variety of printing tasks encountered in a portfolio process. However, bear in mind a caveat when using the PDF format. If your PDF contains a JPEG image it will consistently be larger than the original JPEG file, as the PDF does not further reduce the JPEG size.

WHAT ARE THE
COMPRESSION TOOLS

Bringing your images together into a single printable PDF can result in an enormous file due to the high image resolutions needed for printing. How much to compress your images depends on your selected portfolio format, destination media and even software and device capacities. However, don't sacrifice quality, as it should always be your priority. Strive for the most manageable size while maintaining quality.

DO always store the original image file. You may need it in its original quality and resolution.

To apply compression to your files, you have a couple of alternatives. Image editing software, such as Photoshop or Affinity Photo, already provide a range of compression options. One method in these softwares involves "re-sampling" the image, which essentially repacks the data while adjusting image dimensions or resolution. If you do not want to change the dimensions or resolution, you can re-save a file as a JPEG and choose from various levels of compression. The compression range is wide, and the greater the compression the more you lose data and quality from your image. Always back up original files before trying compression methods, so that you can gauge the loss of quality as well as return to your starting point.

DON'T rely on what you see on the monitor. Always test print.

Another common and widely used alternative is to explore online image compression tools. Websites such as compressjpeg.com, freeconvert.com, or tinyjpg.com, can provide pretty effective "lossless" compression /no loss of data or quality/ of your images. If your images are compressed and your PDF file is still large, next you can try to compress an entire PDF document using these online tools.

WHY COLOR PROFILE MATTERS

Much like selecting an ideal image resolution to achieve print clarity of your images, you will also need to set the proper color profile to achieve the best color representation in your print images. Usually, you will want to print files saved in a CMYK color profile, but understanding why this color mode is recommended might help you assign the right color profiles to your files in the future.

Since print and screen technology are so different, two distinct color profiles have evolved, presenting colors to the eye in different ways. The screen or RGB /red, green, blue/ model pushes color forward with red, green, and blue light dots /pixels/, and the mix of these primary colors achieves the color the eye detects. Full-color light mixes with white, and a lack of lighted pixels reverts to black. This is considered an additive model, adding light to the black screen. The print or CMYK model /cyan, magenta, yellow, black/ is considered a reductive model because it begins with white paper, and printed color dots reduce the white to a mixture of other colors, with the maximum ink or toner color on the page reducing the white paper to black.

Given the distinction between these two color profiles, you likely understand why it is so important to convert your digital files into CMYK when working on editing software. Without this conversion, the RGB colors you see on your screen may appear faded or otherwise inaccurate when you print your screen image to paper. You might consider setting up CMYK at the beginning of your workflow, which will allow you to design with the final print colors from the beginning. Alternatively, you can convert to CMYK later in your design process, but be mindful that color discrepancies are expected and may require time to fix. In case you want to create a portfolio for both mediums, you might consider working with a dual workflow. You can start to design in RGB for a broader color space and periodically check and adjust for how colors will look when converted to CMYK before finalizing for print. It's important to note that some recently manufactured printers can properly handle files with an RGB profile, but this depends on your specific printer or print services. No matter the case, you will want to run test prints long before you finish the printing process to be sure the colors you see back-lit on a screen translate to the printed paper.

DO use a consistent color profile within document for a cohesive appearance.

⎯ DIGITAL PORTFOLIO

WHAT IS A DIGITAL
PORTFOLIO

Before considering the digital process, a distinction should be clearly understood: digital portfolios are still book-like portfolios laid out in a linear page-by-page presentation. Digital portfolios most often take the form of a PDF, which can be either printed or uploaded online. A separate category of digital portfolio involves websites that serve as your portfolio, accessible to the public at any time. As this digital type differs inherently from conventional digital or physical portfolios, the website portfolios will be addressed separately later in this Step.

WHAT ARE THE BENEFITS
OF A PDF PORTFOLIO

The architecture and design industry today moves fast and relies on digital platforms. So, as already emphasized, it is essential that you have a digital portfolio, whether you are applying for academic programs or seeking employment. PDFs are still the widely used and accepted digital portfolio format. They maintain a consistent visual appearance and compatibility across nearly all platforms.

Fortunately, both physical and digital portfolios begin their workflow digitally, which makes it convenient to use the digital version as a precursor to the physical one. If done correctly, the adaptability of a digital PDF portfolio will allow for a seamless conversion from a screen-ready to a print-ready format whenever necessary.

Unlike printed media, a digital PDF portfolio is easy to present as a tailored and updated version of your most relevant projects. This low-effort customization is more cost-effective than constantly printing new copies every time you make an addition or update. Lastly, since the digital landscape has reshaped the way we not only present but also share our work, having an easily shareable digital PDF portfolio allows you to reach a wider audience instantly by uploading it to social media, online platforms, or sending it as an email attachment. This strategic advantage permits prospective employers to quickly and easily get a glimpse of your talent, which can lead to more opportunities and a quicker decision-making process.

Nowadays, most PDF authoring tools offer the ability to add interactive features such as hyperlinks, buttons and multimedia files like audio, video or GIFs into your design. Undoubtedly, these tools elevate the engagement of the audience as opposed to a static PDF. If you choose to pursue this approach, using software like Adobe InDesign could be one option to transform your static PDF into an interactive presentation.

WHAT ARE THE DRAWBACKS
OF A DIGITAL PDF PORTFOLIO

On the flip side of the coin, digital PDFs come with their own set of drawbacks. One of the most notable downsides is the limitation on file size, which can restrict the inclusion of some of your high-quality image files. This constraint may force you to compress data-heavy files, leading to potential image degradation. Additionally, unlike print media, PDFs present less control due to wide variations of user devices and screens, which can significantly change or degrade the overall viewing experience. For instance, while digital portfolios are often designed to be viewed on larger screens, they can still be accessed on smaller devices, where it might be difficult for viewers to fully appreciate your work as well as the intentions and design of your portfolio. Also, keep in mind that depending on the device used to view your work, the appearance of digital colors, brightness and contrast may significantly impact how your portfolio is perceived, undermining the visual integrity of

DON'T expect PDFs to work well on small screens. They have a fixed layout!

DO remember that viewing PDFs on smaller screens requires a lot of time zooming in and out.

58

your work. All things considered, a printed portfolio, indeed, is real and irreducible. However, a digital portfolio, for better or worse, can be viewed on the phone, even in a tight airline seat.

While PDFs do support certain interactive features, they lack the dynamism of web-based platforms. The support for interactive elements may be limited, and complex animations or components may not be well-supported. Given the potential compatibility risks, carefully consider the purpose and accessibility of these features to ensure they enhance rather than detract from the overall experience for your audience.

WHAT ARE PDF ALTERNATIVES

DON'T send your audience a PowerPoint presentation. A PPT file is not a professional standard.

To create a PDF portfolio, designers typically create it with standard tools such as Adobe InDesign, Illustrator, or even Photoshop. However, depending on your circumstances, you may want to use other software instead of the Adobe package subscription, such as Microsoft Publisher or an online tool like Canva, Scribus, or Affinity Publisher. These alternatives offer flexibility in design and may meet your specific requirements.

The alternative that may appeal to many would be Microsoft PowerPoint. This easily accessible software requires minimal effort and a quick learning curve in order to create an impressive presentation fairly quickly. PowerPoint is usually used to build a slideshow that allows for visually engaging presentations. Unlike static PDFs, PowerPoints can easily feature animations, transitions, and interactive elements, making a presentation more lively. However, since your presentation needs to be converted to a PDF, some of the features you applied in PowerPoint may not be transferred, leading to the loss of interactive and multimedia elements.

If you do end up building your PDF portfolio in PowerPoint or other popular and easy-to-use softwares such as Google

Slides, you might be tempted to rely on the pre-made design options provided by the software. While these design choices can save time and effort, their standard nature makes them inappropriate for the professional design field. Similarly, robust customization options offered in these softwares, a variety of colors, sounds, shapes, and other features, may be inviting, but it's easy to go overboard. Remember, PowerPoint templates and default choices are often geared towards a more general, less professional audience.

DO use customization tools sparingly in PowerPoint to prevent compromising accessibility.

PORTFOLIO PROCESS TO SCREEN —

HOW TO OPTIMIZE IMAGES FOR THE SCREEN

Optimizing your images for printing and optimizing your images for the screen can be quite different processes, although many of the tools are the same. If your digital portfolio is intended strictly for the screen, you should follow the image optimization procedures for website images that will be discussed later in this Step. Screen images can be reduced to lower resolutions and still be effective, and it is imperative to reduce their file data size as much as possible to reduce loading times. Also, screen images should be saved strictly as RGB color profiles.

However, if your digital portfolio will also serve a dual purpose and be used for printing a portfolio, your image optimization will be more complicated. You should consider with a dual workflow. Once again, you can begin your design in RGB for a broader color space but make sure to check how print colors will look when converted to CMYK profile. You may end up with two sets of almost identical images, except that one set will be optimized for printing /larger data sizes/ and the other optimized for screen viewing.

*DO check on the
visual integrity of
compressed files
before sharing
with others.*

A daunting procedure can be converting your PDF portfolio
into a share-friendly file, especially with a completed portfolio
spanning 30 to 50 pages, which can be a substantial file size.
Ideally, you want to share your digital portfolio directly and not
send a link to a location such as Google Drive. To overcome
this, try adjusting the compression settings as you save or
export your PDF. If the exported file still remains sizable,
consider uploading it to an online compression tool. This tool
can achieve a lot while maintaining the quality of your images.

— SELECTING A FORMAT

Whether your portfolio takes shape as a physical object or a
digital file, the ultimate goal is to properly present the fullness
of your work in a confined form. With this goal in mind, you need
to start making your initial choices, such as the page size and
orientation of your portfolio — your foundation for the proper
display of your work. All your future design decisions will be
based on these choices, so they need to be considered carefully.

The best place to start is to ask yourself whether you
prefer your portfolio to be viewed in a landscape orientation
/horizontal/ or a portrait one /vertical/. Or, the portfolio
may even take on more unconventional shapes, such as a
square. But be mindful that while unique formats can be more
attractive, they may also require more time and effort.

While you may have the freedom to choose a page orientation
and page size that will display your project in its best light, you
do need to first consider several factors that may constrain
or dictate your decision:

- **audience requirements**
- **professional standards**
- **image dimensions**

Prior to making any initial design choices, you need to prioritize the audience's requirements. There's a possibility that an academic institution or professional firm has already provided guidelines regarding page size and orientation. Therefore, you must conduct thorough research and understand their requirements beforehand.

While there are no specific professional standards for page size, physical portfolios may have some limitations for practical reasons. Sticking with a standard paper size /such as letter, tabloid, A4, A3, or even A5/ can be more economical. Custom sizes may require meticulous trimming of each page, which can be costly and time-consuming. Standard sizes also work well with digital PDF portfolios, even though your portfolio is designed primarily for screen purposes. The standard page aspect ratios often closely match standard computer widescreens, which are typically 16:9.

DO remember that smaller page sizes are more convenient for transport or mailing.

The primary consideration when choosing a format and page size should be your visual content. Take into account the orientation of your renders, drawings, and other visuals, such as photography. While there is no one-size-fits-all solution, select the format that best complements the most pivotal images you intend to present. This approach may accelerate your decision-making and simplify the process as you arrange your images into related proportions. But remember that the size you choose will not only impact the layout and design of your portfolio but also affect the amount of information the viewers will see on each page. Therefore, carefully evaluate the advantages and limitations of the chosen page size and orientation. Take the opportunity to explore sample portfolios to understand how different formats might affect your work.

Or, do quick sketches to understand the proportions' impact on your presentation. Finally, if you have the time, you may want to go forward with a tentative plan and see how it works before fully committing.

WHY USE A HORIZONTAL
LANDSCAPE FORMAT

DON'T force the viewer to rotate your portfolio to be able to comprehend your work.

A landscape format most commonly uses a standard size U.S. tabloid /11x17"/, or A3 /29.7x42 cm/. A horizontal layout offers a wide field that can hold many images with larger dimensions. Its elongated aspect creates a sense of continuity and flow, making it perfect for storytelling, progression, or panoramic images. While it may seem like a landscape orientation is your go-to choice, as the majority of your work may have a square or horizontal aspect, keep in mind that a two-page spread provides you with a very wide field, and therefore, it is easy to visually overload the pages with information. Also, if you're creating a digital portfolio such as a PDF, a horizontal layout will be easier to view on a computer screen rather than a phone since users might have to scroll horizontally to see all the content, which can be a frustrating and unintuitive experience.

WHY USE A VERTICAL
PORTRAIT FORMAT

The vertical portrait format stands out as the most prevalent and easy to work with option. This popularity can be attributed to the cost-effectiveness, with letter size /8.5x11"/ or A4 /21x29.7 cm/ being the favored dimensions. Unlike the expansive horizontal landscape layout, the vertical portrait format offers limited space for your content, which means that you may end up with more pages or perhaps even cluttered layouts. Nevertheless, when used appropriately, this compact vertical format creates an emphasis on the layout composition, resulting in a minimalistic layout that can elevate the imagery. The constrained space also provides

HORIZONTAL FORMAT

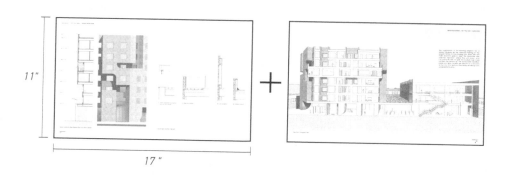

17 "

11"

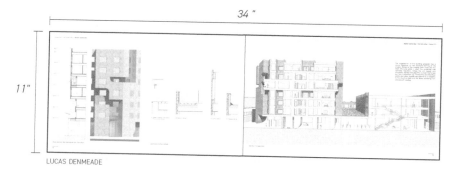

34 "

11"

LUCAS DENMEADE

provides more space
natural viewing experience
sense of continuity and flow
fuller presentation
easy to browse /if a physical copy/

tabloid format

PREVIEW ON MEDIA

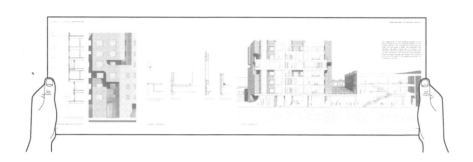

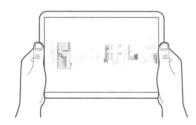

VERTICAL FORMAT

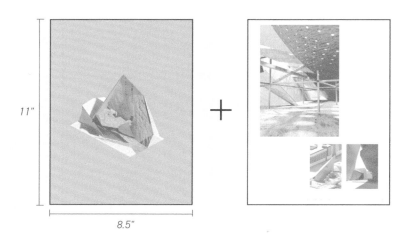

11"

8.5"

17"

11"

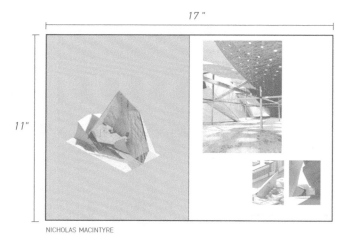

NICHOLAS MACINTYRE

simpler space utilization
focused visual experience
effective cohesion
readability
compact / if a physical copy/

letter format

PREVIEW ON MEDIA

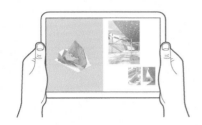

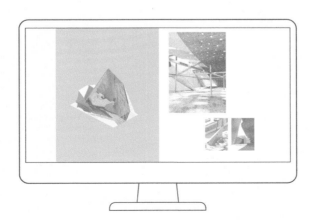

SQUARE FORMAT

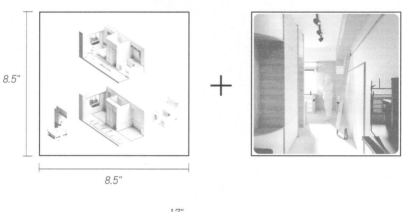

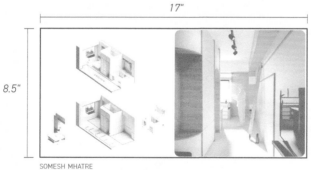

SOMESH MHATRE

contemporary feel
unity and symmetry
effective cohesion
readability
compact / if a physical copy/

square format

PREVIEW ON MEDIA

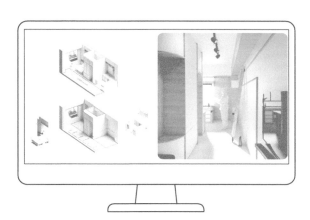

a more focused visual experience for the viewer, allowing them to be attentive to one part at a time. Lastly, for a digital portfolio, a vertical portrait format is obviously suitable for mobile devices. When viewed as a spread of two portrait pages, the layout turns into a landscape format that fits nicely with larger screens.

WHY USE
A SQUARE FORMAT

A less standard yet contemporary square format can add a genuine uniqueness to the overall portfolio aesthetic if you design it well. The most optimal proportions for this format are 8.5x8.5" for letter size and 21x21 cm for A4. A square layout provides balance as the width and height match one another, with a main focus drawn to the center of the page. When opened, the square format can leverage the landscape format as it provides an elongated view. Moreover, due to its equally proportioned dimensions, this format can effectively accommodate both horizontal and vertical imagery. However, compared to other discussed formats, a square provides the least space to work with. While it offers a wide double-page spread, it can be challenging to avoid clutter given its already limited dimensions. Therefore, you have to be especially attentive to give a proper scale to your imagery while giving an appropriate white space around it, and you can expect a longer page count. You might consider using larger squares than 8.5", but this could entail additional costs if you opt for a physical copy. Be aware that the square format will require trimming after printing, as it will be printed on standard paper with a rectangular ratio. This may significantly affect the cost and/or time you need to complete your portfolio.

— ONLINE PORTFOLIO

WHAT IS AN
ONLINE PORTFOLIO

DO remember that anything you share online never disappears.

Although an online presence today seems like a clear necessity, the reality is not as straightforward. While it is an accessible way to gain more exposure for your work, merely posting a portfolio online doesn't automatically guarantee access to your desired audiences, be it prospective employers or architectural programs. However, once you establish a connection with your audience, an online portfolio becomes a powerful way to showcase your architectural skills and potential.

DO consider attaching your portfolio link to your LinkedIn profile or other social media.

In the current professional landscape, it is not unusual for employers to examine the online presence of prospective employees as part of the decision-making process. Given that nearly everyone in contemporary society has some form of online representation, particularly on social platforms such as Instagram, an online portfolio becomes a part of the up-to-date scene. It empowers you to regulate and curate your public image to a certain degree, allowing employers a clearer insight into your identity through your online presentation.

Sharing a direct link with your audience prior to a meeting can be a strategic move that helps to establish a sense of credibility and might facilitate a more productive and successful meeting. Similarly, providing a link when leaving a meeting can encourage your prospective employers to consider your potential more fully, as they can explore a comprehensive collection of your work, achievements, and skills.

However, bear in mind that an online portfolio is a broad presentation of your work that cannot be tailored to each specific firm you apply to. This lack of customization means that you have limited control over which projects are being

71

viewed and emphasized. Therefore, given an online portfolio's broad nature, your audience might only focus on a select few of your works, possibly overlooking your best or most relevant projects. Your online portfolio can take several forms:

• **online publisher**
• **portfolio hosting website**
• **portfolio website**

WHAT IS AN
ONLINE PUBLISHER

The most straightforward and simplest way to establish yourself online is by using your already created digital PDF portfolio. Numerous services provide platforms for hosting your digital portfolio document, and these services are generally affordable, user-friendly, and offer a degree of customization. Online publishers such as Issuu or Yumpu are digital publishers that convert your final PDF portfolio into an interactive online publication that can be effortlessly shared through various digital channels, typically through a direct link. Moreover, some of these platforms will convert your portfolio into an actual page-turning online book, which can be viewed on any device without erratic performance issues. However, as is typical for hosting websites, each of them has its own charges and restrictions, such as a limit on the file size of your portfolio. So be sure to research the various options before you select one.

DO keep in mind that some of the online publisher platforms restrict the file size and the number of uploads.

WHAT IS A PORTFOLIO
HOSTING WEBSITE

If you're short on time or just looking for a quick and effective way to establish an online presence, using a portfolio-hosting website could be a good option. These design community platforms, such as Behance or Dribbble, provide you with a space to display your projects in a gallery-like manner. Not only do these platforms come with built-in social features that make it easy to connect with other professionals and build your reputation, but they also generate a unique URL for easy sharing. While these sites may require a bit more time and effort to set up, the potential benefits of exposure and connectedness may be well worth it. One significant advantage of these sites is that they are marketplace forums where viewers seek out professional work. You'll be in the marketplace.

However, one major disadvantage of using online hosting platforms is that you lose some control over visual presentation and your message or brand. Since these platforms prioritize uniformity and consistency in their display, your unique work becomes submerged within the platform's framework, which reduces the possibility of receiving the attention it deserves. Additionally, you'll recognize early on that when using portfolio hosting platforms, you are not in control of the space you're using. The platform's terms of service and server guidelines often impose restrictions and often dictate how you can present your work, which can significantly and unfavorably impact your presentation.

Another drawback of online hosting platforms is that their primary focus tends to showcase only the final results of projects without attention to process, including rough sketches, diagrams, and different iterations of your designs. While presenting the final outcome is certainly purposeful, it is just as important for the audience to see the project's evolution and the challenges that were overcome. Also, since the sites emphasize exquisite, attention-getting results, trying to compete for attention might reshape your presentation. Often the most valuable advantage of hosting sites resides in the simple, direct link to your online portfolio without a need for attachments or downloads.

WHAT IS A
PORTFOLIO WEBSITE

The most comprehensive online choice is to create your own website — an expressive, semi-permanent, and dynamic platform for showcasing your work. But you should not feel obligated to build one, especially if you're at the early stages of your career or, as an experienced professional, not considering a solo path. Yet, if you do have a substantial body of work suitable for online display, having a website as an architectural portfolio can bring many benefits.

DON'T use auto-playing audio or video on your website. It becomes an intrusive element.

While building a well-functioning portfolio website can indeed be a laborious task, the trade-off is that it unlocks numerous dynamic possibilities and responsive designs that are difficult to achieve with a static PDF or print portfolio. Not only does a website portfolio come with an opportunity to showcase a broad range of your work, it also enables you to integrate interactive content /video, audio, animations/ and modern web design elements such as scrolling effects like parallax. By seizing the opportunity to create a visually appealing, functional, and well-maintained portfolio website, you can significantly enhance your chances of gaining a competitive edge over other applicants. However, remember to negotiate a balance between creativity and functionality. While these dynamic features do allow a higher degree of engagement, an overly complex or poorly optimized website may lead to slow loading times and potential user frustration.

DON'T push creativity at the expense of usability in your website portfolio.

A clear advantage of a website portfolio is your potential to present a diverse range of your projects yet keep a succinct and well-organized overview. The non-linear nature of a website's presentation allows visitors to engage with your gallery of work in an individualized way. This structure also allows you to emphasize your special projects while still offering a depth of overall work. At a micro level, this format will enable you to provide detailed access to your projects, giving you ample space to showcase your thought process and development. With no practical limits on the amount of content or pages and with a thoughtful navigation setup, users have the freedom to choose which projects they want to delve into deeper without the need to browse through all of your images.

DO use keywords, meta descriptions or tags to enhance your SEO /search engine optimization/.

Nowadays, creating and managing a website is more accessible and affordable than ever before. In fact, you don't need to have coding knowledge to build and maintain your own website. Platforms like WordPress, Wix or Squarespace, and Adobe Portfolio provide all the necessary tools /including CMS — content management systems/ to create a website with relative ease. While some platforms come with a cost or require some understanding of website coding, others offer free trials, templates and instructional videos, allowing you to explore and test your potential site before making final decisions. Keep in mind that the cost structure, restrictions, and offerings of the platform services may change over time.

WHAT ARE THE DRAWBACKS OF A WEBSITE PORTFOLIO

DON'T try to build your own website portfolio from scratch if you haven't worked on websites before.

A notable drawback of a portfolio website is the ongoing cost of hosting a domain, which can get pretty expensive. While it's possible to operate a site with your own domain name for less than $200 per year, you need to have technical skills to build and maintain it. Since hosting service prices vary greatly, you need to shop around to avoid paying more, especially if you need a content management system to keep your website up and running. There are options for less expensive alternatives, but they will most likely come with limitations, such as lacking flexible content management tools, fast performance, or security features. And although it might be tempting to consider free domain hosting services, it's better to stay away from them. These services typically come with advertising and pop-ups, which can detract from the professional quality of your portfolio.

DO keep your domain short and simple to make it easy to remember.

A portfolio website introduces a problem that conventional portfolios don't have to face. And that is to develop a simple, intuitive interface for your users. While your audience is familiar with interacting with a physical book, of course, they may wonder which page to navigate to next, what content they should view first or last, and how to seamlessly explore your portfolio. A well-designed interface should have uncomplicated, readily apparent navigation, fast loading times, and accessibility across all devices for all users. The following sections will briefly discuss ways to design an effective website portfolio interface.

DO be cautious using website pre-made design templates. It may be hard to distinguish yourself from the competition.

WEBSITE PORTFOLIO PROCESS —

WHY WELL-STRUCTURED NAVIGATION MATTERS

Having visually appealing content on your portfolio website may sound like the key to making a strong first impression, but it is not enough to guarantee success. While the aesthetics of your website can surely grab attention, the real substance lies in its functionality. If visitors find it difficult to navigate your website, they may quickly lose interest and never return.

DO utilize the benefit of well-structured navigation menus offered by website hosting platforms.

To make navigation easy to use and especially intuitive, begin by making it simple. Your site does not need to be complicated for your work to be impressive.]Your navigation menu should be easily found and easily read. The site structure beyond your homepage can be as simple as project pages and an "about" and "contact" page. Each project can go one, two or three pages deep, depending on the project content you want to share and/ or the viewer's interest. The path to anywhere on the website, including a quick return to the homepage, should be clear and easily accessible. This book focuses on visual composition, but a website portfolio must put functional design first.

DON'T use horizontal scrolling as it creates a poor user experience.

DO optimize images for responsive websites, which sometimes can be data heavy and suffer from slow loading times.

In addition to well-done navigation, you will need to achieve "adaptive design." Having a static website design that only performs well on computer screens is no longer acceptable. Your website must look consistent across various devices because even professionals might view your portfolio website on their phones, at least initially. Fortunately, some hosting platforms like WiX or Squarespace already provide you templates with built-in adaptive or responsive design strategies. They also offer a variety of navigation menus to build from. If you don't make use of the variety of components and templates available today, you will need a good bit of technical skill to code your customized website. However you plan to build your website, you should streamline your workflow by building your website layout with the current range of phone screens in mind and then include tablets and large screens in your designs. This approach will help you assess from the beginning what is visually and functionally required for your website and tailor your content accordingly. Don't complete one screen design and then have to re-think your whole approach.

HOW TO OPTIMIZE
SCREEN IMAGES

Your website imagery not only showcases your aesthetic skills but also serves as a demonstration of your software proficiency and technical knowledge. This proficiency becomes evident through your image optimization to achieve quick loading and a seamless experience. Although image optimization for the web is similar to the optimization discussed for print images, there are sharp differences to understand. Here are the tools and concepts necessary to achieve full, crisp web images:

- image dimensions – pixel width and height
- image quality – resolution
- file formats
- file data size
- compression tools

WHY PIXEL DIMENSIONS
MATTER FOR A SCREEN IMAGE

One of the major differences between a printed portfolio and a screen-based portfolio lies in the resolution. Unlike print, where image quality is contingent on DPI resolution, screen image quality generally depends on the image's overall pixel dimension. Screen width and technology vary from user to user and from desktop to laptop to phone, but the only important resolution number is the total pixels across and down an image and how far those pixels will go on a screen. If your image is 1920 pixels wide and 1080 pixels in height, your image can span with full resolution across a large but standard computer screen of the same dimensions. If the image tries to fill a larger screen with more pixels, the image will degrade. If the image appears on a smaller screen it will either be too big or it will be purposefully compressed and appear clear but smaller.

Once you determine how an image is to be displayed in a layout, then you should have a clear sense of what the pixel dimensions should be for the image. You'll want to save the image at the same pixel width and height as what will appear on the web page. If an image will appear small, say 150 px, it should be saved at 150 px. Don't waste resources loading large images to fill small spaces. When an image is large across a screen, then use your resources to save and load all the necessary pixels.

DO adjust the pixel dimensions to optimize your image for faster page loading.

The issue becomes more complicated when you begin to adapt to different screens. You may have to create multiple layouts for multiple types of screens, and each layout may use the same image in slightly different ways that require differently sized images. Adapting to screens complicates your task, but your goal remains the same. Don't waste resources loading large images to fill small spaces. If you use an image in five different layouts, you may need to resize the pixel dimensions and save five versions of the image.

WHAT IS THE OPTIMIZED SCREEN IMAGE SIZE

Pixel count is a numeric resolution and the resolution of each of your images needs to be verified with your eyes. Depending on how clear the original image was and how the image has been cropped, resized or compressed and in what format it has been saved, the image may or may not have good resolution for the viewer's eye. These matters all need to be considered for quality resolution, while at the same time, you should try to make the digital file that holds the image as small as possible.

For a website portfolio, the image optimization balance — that is, maintaining visual quality while minimizing file data size — must weigh in favor of image quality. Try for speed and ease of use, but never permit reduced quality. Most images for the screen can have a good resolution and not slow down website loading significantly with today's high-speed Internet. If compression does not reduce file data size enough or too much resolution is lost, you should try online compression tools. There are also a few other techniques you can employ for more efficient website loading. JPEG files can be saved as "progressive" images, so they load fully and then come into focus. Or you can try to employ "lazy loading" so images lower on a page don't have to load until needed.

WHY FILE FORMATS
OPTIMIZE SCREEN IMAGES

Understanding the various image file formats and selecting the right ones for your website will lead to the best representation of your work and improve your site's performance. Although there are numerous image file formats in use, the following formats are almost always the most suitable options for optimal browser support and speed:

- **Joint Photographic Experts Group – JPEG**
- **Portable Network Graphics – PNG**
- **Web Picturer forma – WebP**

JPEG has become the standard image file format used by most websites, primarily due to its reliable compression that balances reasonable image quality and file data size. This results in faster loading times compared to other file formats. However, remember that because JPEG has a "lossy" character /that is, some data is lost or sacrificed in the compression process/ your images may not result in crisp detail, which is particularly noticeable in line drawings and text, both leading to poorer text readability.

PNG is another commonly used file format for online use. Two reasons are that it uses a "lossless" image compression, which helps preserve details in lines and supports transparency, allowing you to blend images smoothly if needed. However, the trade-off for its lossless nature is that PNG can lead to larger file sizes, which may negatively impact your website's performance.

WebP is a relatively new image format developed by Google, specifically created to enhance image handling in the web browsing experience. It is specifically designed to help websites load faster by offering better compression than formats like JPEG and PNG while retaining similar quality.

DO "Save for web" when saving your images in image editor software.

Additionally, WebP not only supports transparency but also animations, making it the perfect solution to enhance the visual appeal of your websites. Although some browsers and software do not support it yet, the benefits of WebP's superior compression outweigh the risks. And so, with growing support, WebP is rapidly becoming a standard format for online images.

WHAT ARE THE COMPRESSION TOOLS

DO aim for image sizes ranging from 200–500 KB for a website.

Whether you intend to use compression tools for print or screen optimization, the process is more or less the same. For guidance, refer to the earlier section on image compression tools in the print process section. Bear in mind, though, that images intended for screen use should undergo more extensive compression compared to those intended for print. While quality printed images may have a file data size that is several megabytes, even the largest image on your website shouldn't be more than 200–500 KB if it has been compressed properly.

WHY COLOR PROFILE MATTERS

Similar to how printed colors need to be represented in a CMYK color profile, the images you intend for a screen display should adopt an RGB profile. This practice ensures that the colors in your images are accurately presented to all screen viewers. Since the RGB color profile operates through an additive process, it offers you an opportunity to work with a diverse range of color possibilities, resulting in vibrant and vivid appearances on a screen. If you will not be printing images, you should establish an RGB color profile at the outset of your workflow to leverage the benefits of its vibrant color resolution.

COMMON MISTAKES —

NEGLECTING THE BINDING
PRODUCTION CHALLENGES

Printing a physical portfolio often brings about challenges and limitations, particularly with the binding process. Issues such as placing content near the binding area /see common mistakes 1/, misaligned images spanning across the layout, or improper folding can easily detract from the overall presentation and, at worst, result in the loss of crucial information. Thus, testing your methods or talking with print services when dealing with binding, special image treatment or unconventional print techniques can prevent you from such disappointments.

If you choose to bind your own portfolio, assess your skills, particularly regarding the binding type and its complexity. While creativity is prized in design industries, maintaining a level of professionalism in your portfolio is equally important. Elaborate and engrossing bindings may take away from the seriousness of your work, so it's best to opt for neutral, muted bindings that will most likely align with your audience /see common mistakes 2/.

SLOW
LOADING TIMES

Slow loading times are a frequent issue with many portfolio websites, particularly when these sites do not impose limits on the number of images. While hosting services could be a contributing factor in some cases, the more probable culprit is the large file data size of your images, resulting in sluggish website loading /see common mistakes 3/. This can lead to long waits for visitors browsing your site, causing them to lose interest before even seeing your work. Slow loading underscores the critical importance of image optimization for

DON'T waste resources loading large images. Adapt image sizes to different types of screens.

portfolio websites, particularly in the context of responsive websites, where image optimization holds even greater significance, because it reacts to screen sizes and will. The concept of responsible website behavior is further discussed in Step 5.

Additionally, handling large file sizes can make it challenging to manage, share, load, or even store it. Therefore, always adopt practices reviewed in this Step to reduce the file data size without sacrificing quality. To expand on the optimization techniques, you could also apply a strategy that involves cropping out unnecessary parts of an image. This not only reduces the file data size but also draws attention to the most important details of your image.

LACK OF MOBILE RESPONSIVENESS

DO search for a free browser compatibility test, to see if your website performs smoothly on all standard browsers.

Nowadays, an adaptive design is an absolute necessity. Users don't want distorted layouts with misplaced, overlapped, or even cut-off objects, buttons, and other essential content /see common mistakes 4/. Such an experience will cancel out or badly damage the message you are trying to convey to your audience, leading to lost opportunities. Also, be sure to test your website on different devices to fine-tune its performance and appearance on different screen sizes.

COMMON MISTAKES

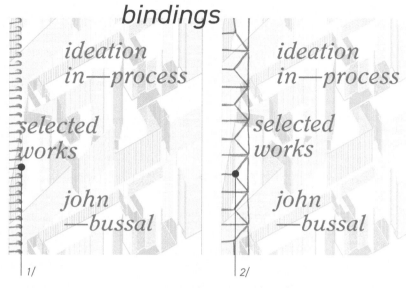

1/ Placing content close to the binding area can cause content distortion and unintended messaging.

2/ Highly elaborate bindings may lack a polished, professional look. Also, they may wear prematurely and tear.

Ensure that the binding doesn't interfere with your content. Choose a binding that aligns with both functional considerations and the desired aesthetic of your portfolio.

ideation
in—process

selected
works

john
—bussal

adaptability

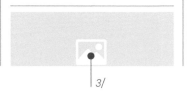

3/

4/

3/ Images with a large file data size may increase the page loading time or, if saved in an inappropriate format, not appear at all.

4/ A website designed only for one screen size may not appear properly, resulting in cut off images, small text and an overall poor user experience.

Your portfolio website must be adaptive. As you develop it, you should steadily test it across different devices to make sure it'll be accessible to all users.

STEP 4

LAYOUT ORGANIZATION

INITIAL SETUP

THEME

— LAYOUT
INITIAL SETUP

The layout of your portfolio page is as crucial as the content it holds. The appropriate compositional arrangement of images and text can improve how viewers interpret, understand, and value the work in your portfolio. Although the content of your portfolio is, in most ways, already determined, you still have full control over the composition and layout. Whether developing a physical, digital or website portfolio, keep in mind that a good layout can enhance understanding and provide visual delight, while a weak layout can cause confusion and lose a viewer's attention and interest. Don't underestimate the importance of the initial layout considerations covered in this Step. They will guide you toward designing your portfolio layout with composition ideas that work for both print and digital media.

— LAYOUT ORGANIZATION

HOW TO APPROACH
LAYOUT ORGANIZATION

DO remember, simplicity is not less creative. It creates focus.

Once you have gathered a selection of your finest work and determined the medium and format you'll be using, you can start building a solid foundation for your portfolio layout. The initial step is to create a layout template that suits your needs and, importantly, brings a unified and consistent appearance to your portfolio.

While you have full freedom to establish a general arrangement of your layout, be mindful to not overload your pages with content. Less is often more, and quality should always be prioritized over quantity. Although your portfolio is a testament to your visual design skill, don't allow any graphics to overshadow your own work. Instead, aim for a layout that is simple, consistent, organized, and yet inventive.

WHY TO PLAN SPREADS
RATHER THAN PAGES

Before you start establishing your layout, it's important to understand that designing a spread, as opposed to individual pages, will make your work easier, more effective, and even immersive. This is especially important with a physical portfolio or any digital booklet version, which are typically viewed in two-page spreads. In such cases, the viewer won't focus on individual pages but rather take in an overall spread. Thinking with a spread-focused approach offers several advantages, including:

> • **planning the design's whole effect at once**
> • **seeing the layout as it will strike the viewer**
> • **detecting layout errors more easily**

WHY TO BE CAREFUL
LOOKING FOR PRECEDENTS

Crafting your own layout composition can prove to be a daunting task, especially if you're not experienced in graphic design. In such cases, it's pretty common to feel overwhelmed and unsure of where to begin. This is when you ought to search for inspiration and look for successful precedents online to spark ideas. While searching for precedents can help, you should be very careful with that strategy. It's very easy to get impressed with examples available online and even end up duplicating someone's style — a style that might already be derivative of an overly popular, over-used approach. So, as you are looking for inspiration online, keep in mind that your portfolio should be your portfolio. Every single decision should feel like it's your own. Therefore, seeking inspiration outside of the architecture field might be a better, safer and fresher approach. Here are some key search terms that can help you find inspiration:

DO use inspirations to develop your own voice.

editorial layout design •
magazine layout design •
booklet layout design •
portfolio design – other than architecture •

HOW TO APPROACH
A VISUAL NARRATIVE

DON'T use pre-made templates for your portfolio layout. They may have a generic appearance.

Before you begin with layout organization, firstly, think about how you can help your audience understand your work while also making it enjoyable for them. To accomplish this, you need to establish a visual narrative, a structural continuity, that guides your audience through your portfolio. Besides the pacing of projects, which you may have already made some preliminary decisions about, a visual narrative also involves critical decisions about how much space and emphasis to give to not only each project but also to each object of your content. These decisions will create a dynamic flow throughout your pages, spreads and the portfolio as a whole. A successful visual narrative should succinctly show your developments and achievements, connect your projects in a compelling story and make clear your distinct approach to your work. To start creating the narrative, organize the portfolio components listed below into thumbnail sketches. This will get you started with a basic outline of your structure.

DO consider implementing section divider pages. They serve as a break and develop rhythm.

cover page •
resume – optional •
design statement – optional •
table of contents •
introductory page project #1 •
project #1 pages •
introductory page project #2 •
project #2 pages•
...
extras – optional •
thank you and contact information •

HOW TO WORK WITH
THUMBNAIL SKETCHES

These days, many begin with software and end with software, and thus design software has become their only tool. While this may work out for some, an initial sketching out of possibilities is an important step that should not be skipped. You may be trying to save time or just avoid the bother, but thumbnail sketches can be a valuable starting point, and bypassing this exploration can lead to broken compositions or simply unfulfilled ones. Whether you prefer to sketch with a pencil and paper or use a drawing tablet, these sketches should be quick, free-flowing, open-ended, and personal glimpses of your ideas. At their best, they are an essential planning tool, allowing you to try out multiple design approaches in a short amount of time.

DO remember, the thumbnail sketches aren't beautiful. They are supposed to be exploratory.

If creating a website portfolio, you may want to consider creating sketches commonly known as wireframes. These wireframes should have the same low-fidelity approach, similar to thumbnails, but with a different purpose. Given the non-linear nature of websites, wireframes should focus on the basic structure, flow, and navigation and may even include responsive design alternatives for various screen sizes.

Your rough, preliminary sketches are usually done within an outlined frame. The frames are ideally placed all on the same page so that you can see the organization, project scope, and page pacing. To avoid getting bogged down in details, it's best to keep the frame proportions small and focus on analyzing the most effective proportions, strategic composition and pacing for each page and the whole document. While creating your thumbnails or wireframes, keep in mind the character of your images. For instance, some may require a large-scale display and some smaller, while others demand a sequential presentation. Also, you may start incorporating rough outlines of other content, such as titles and descriptions, and begin to think of how to place them in the frame. Step 6 will discuss in

DO utilize the thumbnail sketches to see how each page leads to the next.

DON'T restrict your table of contents to one page if it results in a cluttered layout.

depth how to make your layout the most effective. Additionally, establishing separate but cohesive options for each of several project scenarios will effectively demonstrate your layout's usefulness and flexibility /see diagram on the next page/.

Lastly, don't be afraid to make quick decisions and experiment with different variations. If the placement, scale or organization of your content doesn't work, revise it or start again. You are sketching — discovering — not finalizing. The goal is to create a layout design that achieves balance, unity and a narrative-driven experience. Sketches will streamline your process.

— INITIAL SETUP

WHERE TO START
INITIAL SETUP

DO use master pages for folios and running headers. It will save you lots of time.

When building a portfolio, it's essential to work with the right tools. There are various design editing programs available to create print, digital and website media. To begin, you'll be best off selecting a design and layout software that you are comfortable with. Adobe InDesign has become the popular option, perhaps the industry standard, due to its ease of multi-page management and complete layout control for print, digital PDF, or even a website portfolio. If you're not familiar with Adobe InDesign, you can use, for example, Microsoft Publisher, Affinity Publisher, Scribus or an online tool such as Canva. The key is to use software that allows you to work with multiple page layouts at the same time, making it easy to arrange and organize all the content consistently across numerous pages. If your chosen software permits a coordinated multi-page approach, your workflow will be more efficient.

THUMBNAILS EXAMPLES

print media

If using a section divider place it just before each project Intro page.

Cover page   *Intro, Resume*

Table of contents

Intro pages project #1   *Project #1 spread 2*   *Project #1 spread 3*

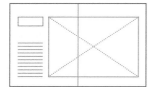   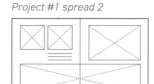   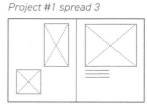

Intro pages project #2   *Project #2 spread 2*   *Project #2 spread 3*

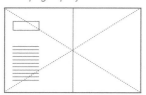   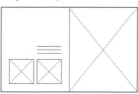   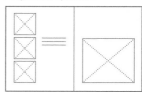

Extras   *Thank you, Contact*   *Back cover*

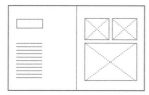   

website media

Homepage

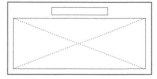

About me, Contact page

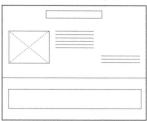

Gallery page

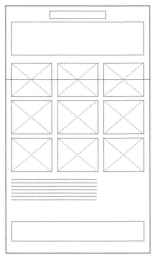

Project page

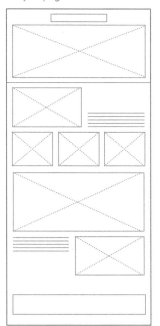

Some prefer tools such as Adobe Photoshop, Illustrator, or Affinity Designer to build their portfolio. If you are creating a short sample portfolio, these tools might work well. However, it may take more time, effort, and skill to achieve a cohesive arrangement and polished look because these image editing softwares are not designed for complex yet cohesive multi-page workflows. For this reason, it's worth considering using or even learning Adobe InDesign, as this software is often a required skill for client presentations. So, it's best to start using it sooner rather than later.

DON'T use Microsoft Word for designing your portfolio layout as it has limited design capabilities.

THEME —

HOW TO
APPROACH A THEME

Once you have determined the preliminary pace and organization of your layouts, as well as your layout editing software, let's continue with the implementation of visual design principles that will bring your portfolio theme alive. First and foremost, it's important to know that a theme is not just about the layout or placement of your objects. A theme is a style that will deliver and highlight your work through a grid structure, composition, color tone and even typeface selection. Establishing a good theme, or the lack of one, will affect how the viewers gauge your work and ultimately value you as a creative professional.

Therefore, while you begin to imagine your theme and perhaps get tempted by the excitement of customization, you should first know that the strength of your layouts lies in visual principles. These tools create effective and functional communication beyond aesthetic appeal. So, even though you might be tempted to design with elaborate arrangements, excessive use of color, and superfluous graphics, remember that such an approach might give the impression that you prioritize style over your work. As a matter of fact, adding a style to your portfolio as your self-expression is not something you should force but rather allow to naturally arise from your portfolio. The portfolio's quality should derive from the content of your projects and your discerning curation and structure, wherein your visual sensibilities are embedded. Therefore, use the following layout elements and their design principles to support your imagery, strive to highlight particular pieces of your work, and effectively communicate your message.

WHAT ARE THE
LAYOUT ELEMENTS

While the next Steps discuss each element in detail, you first should understand the overall purpose of recognizing and using these elements. The layout elements are meant to help you design your content so it is both visually appealing and easy to navigate, so the quality of your work shines through. By following the principles of these layout elements, you can ensure that your work doesn't push against itself or fall apart but instead works together to convey the intended message and create a positive user experience. To understand layout elements, they can be grouped into three types:

invisible layout elements •
visual layout elements •
textual layout elements •

Even though these layout elements are considered separately over the next three Steps, they are closely related and interconnected in determining the overall visual experience. As the Steps of this guide address each of these elements, they may seem disconnected or unclear in their effects. But, when combined, all the elements shape the final appearance and give force to both your design, your content, and your story.

STEP 5

RULE OF THIRDS

MARGINS

WHITE SPACE

GRID SYSTEM

COMMON MISTAKES

— LAYOUT
INVISIBLE ELEMENTS

While the term "invisible" might suggest hidden meanings or maybe the use of transparencies, the term actually refers to creating an experience in design that works functionally and visually without being noticed. Though these layout elements are unseen, they actually form the foundation of your layout — perhaps the framework, too. In construction, you can't build much of a house without a solid foundation or a frame, even if most people don't see them. Likewise, in layout design, it is crucial to establish a solid base that gives strength and unity. Even though viewers don't see the foundational system, it provides them an effective communication that may not need much additional design or decoration. In fact, the best design often is the invisible. This Step will guide you on how to achieve this type of design.

WHAT ARE THE
INVISIBLE LAYOUT ELEMENTS

DO use a grid. It eliminates random decision-making.

Invisible layout elements are essentially a set of hidden lines that form the underlying framework of your layout. These lines help you arrange, align and focus the page contents, such as images and text, in relation to each other. Apart from organizing content, the guidelines also create passive voids that actively contribute to the overall system structure. The invisible elements that are considered to be a starting point for each composition are:

rule of thirds •
margins •
white space •
grid system •

RULE OF THIRDS —

WHY USE THE
RULE OF THIRDS

While you may need to establish a more complex grid system for your layout to accommodate all of your content, the rule of thirds provides a good starting point to understand fundamental compositional principles. The rule of thirds is a simple but effective grid which naturally creates focal points in well-balanced compositions. Essentially, this concept helps you to decide the best placement of key elements within a frame in order to give each one a visual weight or a visual priority.

To implement the rule of thirds, you first need to prioritize your content so that you understand what you want the viewers to pay attention to first, your key objects. Then you divide your layout into three rows and three columns equally spaced out. Those four points where the row and column dividing lines intersect are known as focal points and serve as natural guideposts for placing your pivotal images and other supportive content. Anchoring your key objects at or near these focal points draws the viewer's attention in a naturally eye-pleasing, yet strong way. Lesser objects then stand off from the focal points in a balanced way. This is how the rule of thirds helps create a sense of visual hierarchy and natural spacing that facilitates the viewer's eye to move between the content objects more easily and intuitively.

DO apply the rule of thirds to your layout to create a sense of visual hierarchy.

Even though this method is simple to implement, it's usefulness is worth remembering and can be effective to use even in the most complex grid layout.

— MARGINS

DON'T place detailed or important content too close to the spine when you are designing a printed book.

Establishing proper margins from the start is essential when designing a layout grid. Margins are one of the primary components of a grid and act as buffer zones between the edge of the page and its content. Essentially, they serve as a border around the page /see diagram/. One of the many roles of margins is to prevent content from being placed too close to the edge of the page or screen, which can become visually discomforting and risks allowing content to get cut off during printing. To determine the size of margins, consider that margins that are too narrow can make a page look dense, which negatively impacts readability. On the other hand, margins that are too wide can sometimes make the page feel under utilized or empty, depending on the content used. Therefore, to create an optimal balance between page content and the negative space of margins in a print or digital PDF, set margins to 0.5 inches from each side. You can choose a narrower margin but 0.25 inches should be the minimum since this margin can make your page hard to read, or, as mentioned, the content can be trimmed off during the printing. Additionally, be aware that some binding methods, such as perfect-bound, can cause content to get lost in the inside margin, depending on the number of pages in your document. Therefore, leave the inside margins a little larger to avoid this issue.

DON'T just design within margins. Instead, design your margins.

While you ought to explore your own margins to see which works harmoniously with your page size, there are some considerations to keep in mind when setting up your margins:

the bottom margins can be wider, to include page numbers •
the inside margin should be wider for some bindings •
the margins should be consistent on all pages •

Adopting margins should also be on your mind when working with various content within your page, particularly when it comes to text. In that case, a margin is also considered a safe zone or quiet border that ensures the integrity and clarity of your content /see Step 7, common mistakes/. Therefore, when you are placing your text, or other important objects such as legends, make sure you provide adequate space around the content to make it easy on the eyes of your audience.

DO keep in mind, margins don't have to be symmetrical.

HOW SCREEN
MARGINS VARY

In website portfolios the margins are perceived as spaces that exist between the content border and the edges of the screen. These spaces are determined by either fixed values that adapt at different breakpoints related to screen width, or scaling values that respond dynamically to the screen size. The screen margin widths should vary depending on the screen size, with larger screens accommodating wider margins and smaller screens having more narrow margins. Margins can be set at a scaling percentage of screen space, each margin set somewhere between five and ten percent of the screen window for a steadily adjusted proportion. For fixed values mobile screen margins can be set to 16 px, in some occasions to 24 px. For tablet screens 24–32 px margins would be appropriate. Laptop or desktop screens can accommodate margins starting from 32 px, and can expand as screen resolution expands. However, similar to the print design, remember that these values are not strict norms. Don't be afraid to experiment with different margin widths to find the appropriate balance that complements your layout and highlights your work.

— WHITE SPACE

WHAT IS
WHITE SPACE

*DO remember
that white space
isn't just about
aesthetics; it also
serves a functional
purpose.*

When creating your layout, you should consider not only the content but also the non-content, the empty space, or, that is, the white space. White space is the area left intentionally empty between the content objects in your layout. Though it may seem counterintuitive to pay attention to or even intentionally create blank spaces in your grid layout, these spaces are just as crucial as the text and images in your design. White space, also known as negative space, provides each object with breathing room, allowing it to stand out. Thus, it is paramount to use your best visual instincts to give each object on the page enough room to maintain a balance between its own positive space and the surrounding negative space. Moreover, white space creates opportunities for your eyes to rest and move smoothly between the other objects in the composition. Incorporating white space into your design will not only enhance the viewer experience through improved readability and clear navigation, but it will also elevate the aesthetics of your overall design. Don't underestimate the power of this design element. It's not there — but it's an integral part of any successful grid system!

While not enough white space can make your layout look cluttered and busy, too much can also be harmful. Overuse of negative space can bury your objects, or other times such layouts can feel incomplete. Strive for balance and use your instincts when it comes to proportioning and spacing. Also, it is important to realize that having large empty spaces in the middle of your layout can create a "hole effect" that distracts the viewer from the content. To prevent this, avoid creating areas of white space centered within or surrounded by other objects.

GRID SYSTEM —

WHAT IS
A GRID SYSTEM

A grid is a matrix of established lines that typically run horizontally and vertically in evenly paced intervals. The vertical lines organize elements such as margins and columns. Margins, as already discussed, hold the space at the outer edges of the grid, while columns are the vertical spans divided by gutters within the page. Across the vertical columns, horizontal flowlines divide the page into horizontal spans or, simply, rows. The intersections of vertical columns and horizontal flowlines create modules. Then the modules can expand across any number of columns or down so many rows and adjust with the grid's dimensions. This allows for a flexible and versatile layout that can accommodate various design needs.

WHY THE USE OF
GRID IS ESSENTIAL

A grid ensures a consistent structure throughout the pages of your document. Most importantly, an established grid system helps to streamline your workflow by ensuring that all the content and margins are more easily sized, aligned, and placed uniformly throughout your portfolio. If planned well, a grid system will give order but also be flexible enough to allow you to adjust and rearrange content as needed. This flexibility is especially important in a project like portfolio design, where you need to be able to customize the layout to your specific requirements.

DO remember that a well-organized grid should be essentially invisible. It should be your guide and not a constraint.

DO remember columns and modules can hold white space as well as content.

You may not have been aware, but the thumbnail sketches you created earlier could have already established a sense of grid. This is because the various facets you are were working with, like the size of your images, the format and orientations of your portfolio, or even the required content on project pages, had already suggested some initial grid lines. Therefore, whether the grid structure examples listed below resemble your implied grids or inspire new design ideas, keep in mind that these samples are just examples. Invest some time experimenting to figure out the grid that suits your content's needs. The basic grid structures that you should consider are:

block grid •
column grid •
modular grid •
hierarchical grid •
fluid grid /website only/ •

Block grid is a popular grid format due to its simplicity. It consists of a large rectangular area that occupies most of the layout's space. In portfolio design, the block grid is frequently utilized on cover pages to display a single image. In other instances, the block grids are effective for square formats where the primary text or image can stand out predominantly framed with open wide margins. The uniformity of the block grid helps to create a sense of balance and stability, making it easier for the audience to focus on the content.

GRID ANATOMY

print media

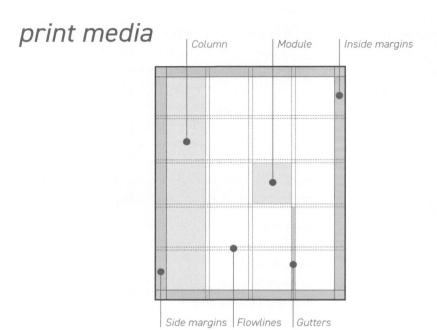

Column | Module | Inside margins

Side margins | Flowlines | Gutters

online media

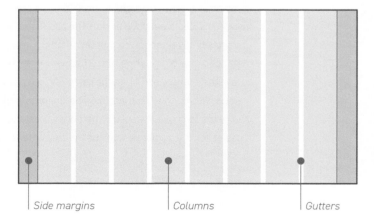

Side margins | Columns | Gutters

GRID EXAMPLES

*Block grid with
wide asymmetrical
margins.*

 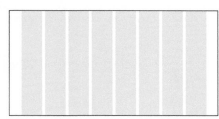

*Column grid with
asymmetrical
and symmetrical
column width.*

 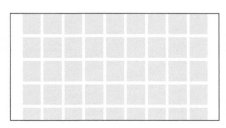

*Modular grid
with square and
rectangle modules.*

 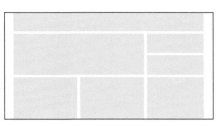

*Hierarchical grid
with different
hierarchal
divisions.*

GRID EXAMPLES

block grid

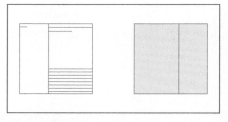

EISH AHLAWAT

*Block grid modified with
a split within.*

column grid

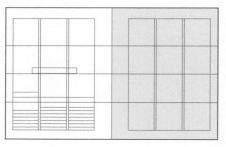

ABDAL KARIM RABI

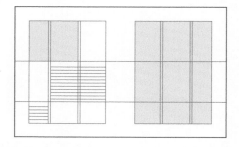

THIAGO LEE

modular grid

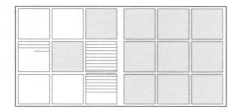

DENIS ZIMAKOV

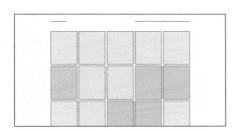

BAND ARCHITECTURE

hierarchical grid

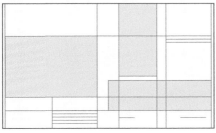

ILIA ALADOV

WHAT IS
A COLUMN GRID

A column grid is made up of at least two columns. If it has more than two columns, it is referred to as a multi-column grid. Multi-column grids are ideal for organizing complex content since they offer a lot of flexibility in creating different layouts. This variability is achieved through the horizontal flowlines, which act like a subordinate structure. These lines can create unique moments in the grid, such as breaking the column to place content anywhere within the column grid or spanning several columns across your layout. It's worth noting that columns can also have different widths, enabling an asymmetrical and dynamic design.

DO understand: the more columns you add, the more flexible your grid becomes.

WHAT IS
A MODULAR GRID

The modular grid divides the layout into columns and rows to create equally sized, rectangular modules. Although it may take some time to learn how to use this grid effectively, it is widely used in portfolio design because it offers the most flexibility. This modular approach allows for creative experimentation by variously combining modules to generate large fields. By joining modules in different ways, each layout can have its unique rhythm while maintaining a cohesive design. The flexibility of a modular grid brings you two benefits. First, you can establish a sophisticated hierarchical structure, and second you can rearrange content easily, which also simplifies portfolio customizing or updating.

WHAT IS
A HIERARCHICAL GRID

Sometimes, the content requires a unique grid system that cannot be met by any of the grid layouts mentioned so far. In such cases, a hierarchical grid can be used. The primary aim of a hierarchical grid design is to first follow the needs of

DO consider an off-center grid, which can be more aesthetically pleasing.

the content. Such a grid consists of columns and rows with varying sizes and intervals. To create this hierarchical grid, you begin by assigning importance to your content, and then you proportion your grid sections and intuitively place objects within the grid in different positions. Because this system is fluid, it can be difficult to apply and requires a trained eye and steady evaluations. To give a polished, refined look to a hierarchical grid, you should establish a rationalized structure that will coordinate or lead the content placement ensuring a cohesive visual flow. In some cases, a hierarchical grid may adopt aspects of two different types of grids to reinforce a strategic approach. Adapting a modular grid, in fact, might be a more reliable framework for hierarchy as it provides structure with flexibility.

WHAT IS
A FLUID GRID

Grids are an especially useful tool for website portfolios, given the potential for chaotic web design. Grids function much the same way on a web page as in a PDF or printed portfolio, except that the web grid is mostly shaped by columns to deal with the vertical nature of a web page. And one other very critical difference: web grids must change constantly depending on the user's screen.

A fluid grid contracts or expands seamlessly to meet the dimensions of the user's screen /or viewing window, known as a "viewport"/. The advantage of a fluid grid is that it maintains the same content and, mostly, the same appearance as it responds to the viewer's screen size. However, this grid system demands a thoughtfully composed layout that can maintain its visual sense despite a dramatic contraction or expansion of its overall viewing field. Two other web grid systems respond to variable views with different strategies. An adaptive grid system creates several fixed grids, with cohesive features

STANDARD GRID SPECIFICATIONS

375 px

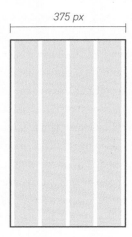

744 px

A mobile device with a screen width of 375 px typically has a four-column grid with side margins set to 16 px and gutters to 12 px.

A tablet device with a screen width of 744 px typically carries an eight-column grid with side margins set to 24 px and gutters to 16 px.

1920 px

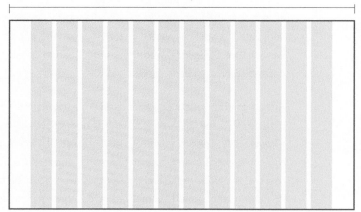

A laptop and desktop screen of the width of 1366–1920 px typically carries a twelve-column grid with side margins at a minimum of 32 px and gutters at 16 px.

GRID BEHAVIOR

fixed behavior

*The fixed grid keeps the content
static, while the margins are scaled
to fill the remaining space.*

fluid behavior

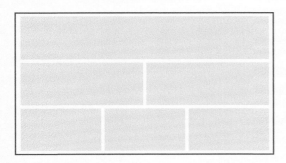 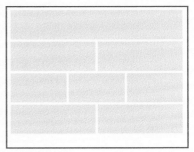

*The fluid grid automatically adjusts
column widths to fill the available
space, while the margin and gutter
widths remain constant.*

but different overall sizes, so an appropriately sized version of the page will appear for the user. A responsive grid is in some ways a combination of fluid and adaptive grids. Some grid elements and content may respond fluidly to window resizing, but at certain breakpoints the grid layout is reformed to better fit a new size. The main point to understand with web layouts is that they need to be size-shifting in some way. Therefore a simple grid is probably best to bring visual order to the complex adjustments required.

HOW TO SET UP
YOUR GRID SYSTEM

When selecting a grid for your layouts, you should pay attention to your content. Your imagery has its own qualities and nature that may dictate your grid system. For example, your imagery may tend toward the horizontal orientation or it may be you have several sets of small sequential drawings. Or for some, your final curation involves large, color-intensive visualizations.

Another aspect to understand about your content is what you want to prioritize. This involves identifying the most important content and what's less important. Once you have a sense of the hierarchy of your content along with the nature of your imagery, then you select a grid that meets your content needs as well as your graphic skills.

Now that you selected your grid, set it up with guidelines that you can easily turn on and off in your editing software. Then start organizing your content accordingly, perhaps with your high-priority imagery first. The grid system will be a visible element at the start, and as you align content with it, you begin to see effects that will last when the lines disappear. While using the grid as the only means of achieving strong consistency is not wrong, it may lead to a monotonous and less engaging viewing experience. Therefore, use the grid

DON'T stick to the grid too strictly. This can lead to uninspiring, homogeneous layouts.

as a starting point for your composition and then customize it to create a more dynamic, personalized scheme that fits your content and overall project. This requires a deeper understanding of the relationship between vertical spans and horizontal flowlines, but with experience, you'll have greater control over your design and confidently break the rules in a reasonable way. For example, you can consider varying the layout from one spread to another, changing the proportions and positions of your images for a more dynamic visual pace. However, while making these changes, maintain a cohesive system by adhering to your base grid. For instance, this book that you are reading is designed with a strong two-column grid, but when content objects need to interrupt the scheme, they are allowed to do so while still maintaining the cohesive feel. Below are some other techniques and recommendations to help you create a dynamic mood for your grid structure while achieving a coherent layout:

combining •
layering •
bleed •
crossover •

HOW TO DESIGN
WITH COMBINING

DON'T fill every single grid module with your content as it can result in an overwhelming visual experience.

A simple and commonly used method to break out of a grid while maintaining a cohesive structure is to combine multiple grid modules. This usually involves removing the gutters to allow content objects to span across two or more columns and perhaps several rows. An object could span a dozen or so modules down and across, depending on its size and the grid structure you use. A similar option is to run your content through the margins, which is known as the partial or full-bleed technique, which will be discussed shortly.

BREAKING GRID EXAMPLES

combined six modules
with elimination of gutters
and margin

combining

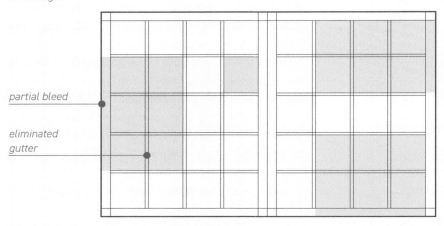

partial bleed

eliminated
gutter

a small object layered
on top of the larger
object

layering

layering effect

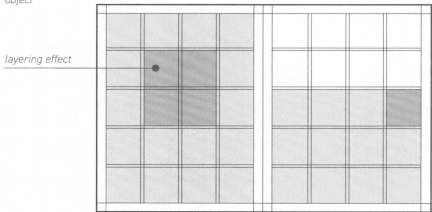

bleed

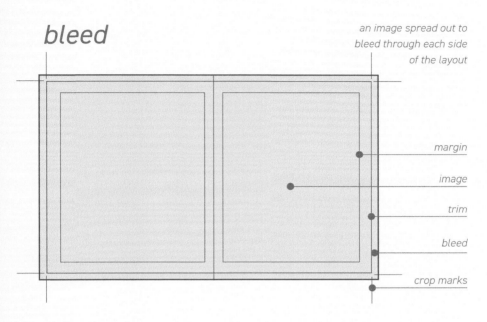

an image spread out to
bleed through each side
of the layout

margin

image

trim

bleed

crop marks

crossover

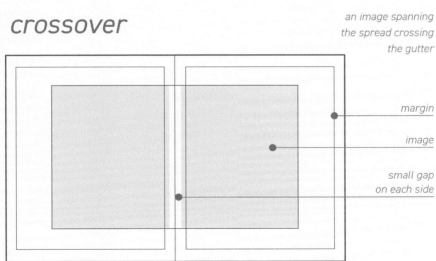

an image spanning
the spread crossing
the gutter

margin

image

small gap
on each side

When combining your modules or collapsing your gutters, it might be tempting to fill up every single available module with your content. Trying to use all the modules, however, leads to a cluttered and overwhelming layout. Though needs vary and a lot depends on how much content you need to fit into your layout, you should always integrate white space to emphasize just one or two objects of your content. The white space you leave becomes a design tool to focus your content.

HOW TO DESIGN
WITH LAYERING

Layering is another technique that can be used to effectively break the monotony of a grid layout. It involves placing one object on top of another, creating an overlay effect that can enliven the viewer's experience. This technique, however, can be challenging to implement as it requires careful consideration of each object's placement, contrast, and readability. If poorly implemented, the layering can be confusing or chaotic for a viewer because objects can blend and become indistinct. So if you lack confidence in your visual instincts or are untrained, it is better to keep the grid simple until you feel more confident.

DO remember that the layering technique can convey an uncertainty about what's important.

If you decide to adopt the layering technique, you will need to experiment and make adjustments to achieve the desired result. For example, if you're layering a floor plan over another image, you'll need to ensure proper contrast to make the floor plan readable. In other cases, you may need to place text on top of a solid or somewhat transparent color block that partially covers the image, creating a sense of unity without compromising the clarity of any of your content /see Step 7, common mistakes/.

HOW TO DESIGN
WITH BLEED

DO consider "break pages" designed with full-bleed images to create a pause, a moment for breath.

A bleed is when an image extends beyond the edge of the page. This way of disrupting a grid system is particularly used in print design, where the image can spread from edge to edge of a page without the interruption of any white borders /margins/. There are two types of bleed layouts: partial bleed, where only a portion of the visual content extends beyond a page edge, and full bleed, where the visual object covers the entire layout, eliminating all the margins. Going full-bleed with an image will not only emphasize your image but also create a unique, immersive moment in your portfolio, drawing the viewer's eye and encouraging a pause to fully appreciate the image's details.

If using a bleed technique, you should understand that the printing process must use sheets of paper larger than the actual page size, which are then trimmed down to the exact size. To ensure that the visual content goes all the way to the edge of the printed paper, always extend your visual content at least 1/8" beyond the final trim size. This guarantees that the images won't leave an undesired white edge on the printed paper.

HOW TO DESIGN
WITH CROSSOVER

A crossover is a technique that gives you an opportunity to create a dramatic effect, but it can be only applied in print design. This method allows for the seamless extension of your content across two adjacent pages by utilizing the grids on both pages. The idea is to violate the constraints of a single page, but of course, this effect only works with pages that face each other. If executed correctly, incorporating crossover images into your layout can amplify the impact of your work, turning images into a more engaging experience.

Achieving a crossover effect requires a lot of consideration to prepare the document for printing. First off, you should avoid having the image's focal point appear at or near the crossover. Secondly, you need to pay special attention to the binding technique used, as it can affect the smooth flow of your crossover image. To avoid the problem of losing too much of an image in the binding fold, you may want to allow narrow margins at the spine. These gaps, or binding margins, allow for a more seamless transition between pages, as they help to prevent any overlap or obstruction that might occur during the binding process. When the pages are bound together, these gaps become practically unnoticeable, and even if some of these interior margins show slightly, the flow of the image is preserved. The size of the necessary gap will vary depending on the binding method and the number of pages in your portfolio. Therefore, it's always best to consult with your printer to ensure that your design is formatted correctly.

DO remember the viewer's eye falls on the right-hand page first. So, in a bound portfolio, use the left-hand page for secondary images.

COMMON MISTAKES —

POORLY DEVELOPED GRID LAYOUT

Setting up the block grid as your primary grid for your portfolio layout is often the go-to choice. While it may be easy to set up since it doesn't require any elaborate divisions, it can easily stifle your creativity and leave your layouts feeling uninspired /see common mistakes 1/. Remember that a block grid is a good choice for cover designs, but it may not offer the necessary structure to create a proper visual hierarchy. With a straightforward block grid, you may have difficulty balancing and visually supporting the whole range of content incorporated in your portfolio layout. Therefore, think about developing your grid further by adding, at the least, more columns to make the layouts more variable and engaging.

On the other hand, when establishing a grid layout, it may seem like a good idea to arrange your content randomly to make it look dynamic and unconventional. However, if your eyes are not trained for composition, this could result in a layout that appears chaotic and confusing, making it difficult for viewers to understand the logical flow and hierarchy of information /see common mistakes 2/. For this reason, it may be better to stick to a structured grid arrangement that promotes consistency.

LACK OF
NEGATIVE SPACE

DO manage the use of white space the same way as your content.

One of the most common mistakes in portfolio design is to try to fill every available space with content. Remember that negative space is just as crucial as the content itself. A composition with content crammed together can seem overwhelming and suffocating, and none of your objects will stand out /see common mistakes 3/. In such a case, viewers are going to struggle to distinguish images and be unable to process the message of your layout. So, don't forget that white space can boost the overall appeal and functionality of your design.

While overlapping images can create a stylish and sophisticated design, you should use this technique cautiously. Overuse or improper application may lead to visual noise and to confusion. The information of your images will be hard to identify /see common mistakes 4/. If your aim is just to squeeze more images on one page, it's better to stay away from this technique. Instead, consider relocating some images to another page or determining which image is most important and giving it the space it deserves without overlapping. Alternatively, you can eliminate an image altogether.

NEGLECTING
THE SAFE ZONE

Narrow margins can deliver modern aesthetics if they are applied with a sensible eye. However, if you're inexperienced, using narrow margins can often lead to counterproductive results. When text and images are placed too close to the edge of your design, it can make your layout appear crowded, unbalanced, and visually uncomfortable for the viewer /see common mistakes 5/. Don't underestimate the importance of setting appropriate margins that provide enough space so that your objects and layout breathe and create visual comfort for the viewer. Additionally, if working on a physical copy, bear in mind that any content too near the edges may get cut off or pushed too close to the binding. So, don't let narrow margins spoil your hard work.

As previously explained, gutters are the spaces between content that prevent images from bumping into each other. Without this visual separation, your content can become crowded and images difficult to distinguish from one another /see common mistakes 6/. Likewise, neglecting a visual gap between text and an image can make the reading unpleasant and cause eye strain. Don't forget about gutter spacing as a part of your design!

DO establish consistent spacing and alignment between like objects.

INCONSISTENT
GRID ELEMENTS

Some designs may require complex grid structures to accommodate a wide variety of content, while others may intentionally have inconsistent grids. Balancing creativity with consistency can be a challenging task in both scenarios and can lead to difficulties in maintaining a cohesive layout. If you have limited graphic design experience, therefore, it might be better to maintain uniform column widths and gutters to ensure that all your objects are aligned correctly in a coherent and organized appearance. Failure to do so may lead not to a uniquely creative result but an unbalanced, unprofessional, and especially confusing viewing experience for your audience /see common mistakes 7 and 8/.

CROSSOVER
DEFECTS

DON'T use bleeds or crossovers without talking to the printer first.

If you are making a physical portfolio and you plan to utilize a crossover technique for your image, it's imperative to format it correctly to achieve the desired effect. Be careful not to place at the binding crossover any critical elements of the image, such as text, legends or focal points. Doing so can obscure or distort the objects and make it harder for the viewer to understand the content /see common mistakes 9/. In such cases, it's better to reposition or crop the image to avoid hindering or distorting the vital information.

Also, be aware of the fact that a spanning image might end up with a misalignment that becomes noticeable once the bound book is opened /see common mistakes 10/. This is because the binding process can cause a small shift in the positioning of the pages. A misalignment is likely to be very slight — but probable — and, therefore, always consult with your printer, who can help minimize this effect and ensure that the image remains as seamless as possible.

COMMON MISTAKES

grid layout

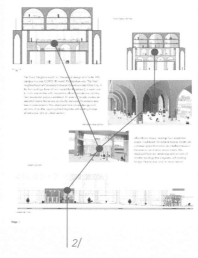

1/ A grid layout that's too basic and rigid can limit the flexibility needed for visually dynamic designs.

2/ Randomly arranged content objects may compete for attention, creating a confusing and less cohesive composition.

Utilizing a more complex yet simple grid can help you to create visually stimulating compositions that maintain both balanced organization and clear focus.

IMAGES THIS PAGE BY CHRISTOPHER MATHES

negative space

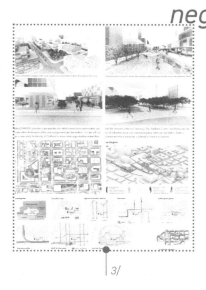

3/

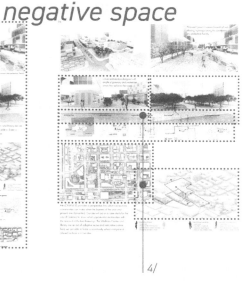

4/

3/ A layout that lacks white space
can make content objects vie
for attention and overwhelm the
viewing experience.

4/ Content objects that overlap may
hinder clarity of your images and
can seem equivocal.

*Negative space can function to
your advantage. Relocating to
another page or even eliminating
some content objects to prevent
clutter helps the viewers perceive,
prioritize and navigate the content
effectively.*

COMMON MISTAKES

safe zone

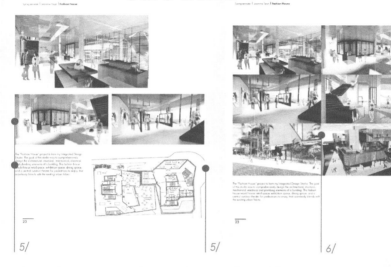

5/   5/   6/

5/ Margins that are too narrow can lead to a crowded layout, inducing visual fatigue and discouraging full engagement with the content.

6/ The absence of visual separation between content objects poses a challenge in distinguishing each from each or focusing on specific content.

Safe zones are visual separations from edges and other content ensure each object is distinct. Your viewer can more easily engage with and interpret your content. Also, when your content object approaches the margins, always consider either extending it to the edge or maintaining an appropriate margin.

IMAGES THIS PAGE BY CHRISTOPHER MATHES

inconsistency

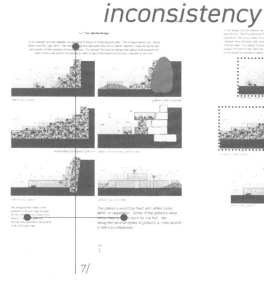

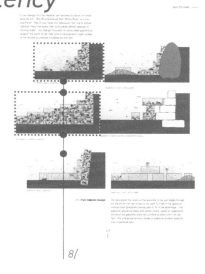

7/

8/

7/ Inconsistent font formatting and paragraph widths create visual chaos and can lead to confusion about the hierarchy.

8/ Varying image sizes and the spacing between them convey a negligence or lack of attention to detail.

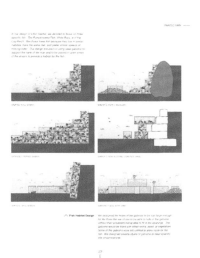

Maintaining uniformity with your gutters, object scale and positions, and typography will elevate your portfolio's overall aesthetics. Not only will it be more pleasing to look at but your message will be clear.

COMMON MISTAKES

crossover

Cabinet of Curiosities

| 9/

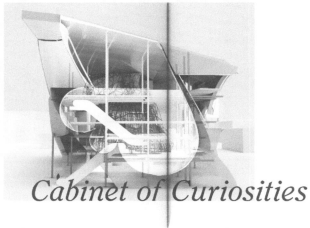

Cabinet of Curiosities

IMAGE BY EVAN BLUEMEL

9/ Placing important information at the spine might result in obscuring it or losing it all together due to the binding.

Reposition or crop the image so the crucial parts are not compromised. Similarly, when dealing with text, adjust the font size or add spacing near the spine to make it readable.

Cabinet of Curiosities

10/

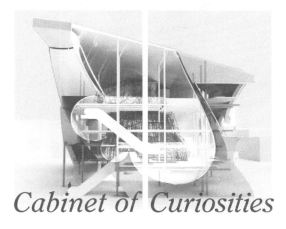

Cabinet of Curiosities

10/ With a bound book, a crossover image might not align properly, causing distortions in both the image and text.

Add an inside margin, try offsetting the images or discuss the other solutions with your print service to improve the continuity of your spanning content.

STEP 6

— LAYOUT
VISUAL ELEMENTS

Visual layout elements play a crucial role in portfolio design because, in part, they attract the most attention. These elements refer to the methods and tools used to create arrangements on a grid that convey a specific message, a message otherwise known as your layout design. All of the image-based content in your portfolio acts as building blocks in these arrangements. These include all visuals such as renderings, drawings, info-graphics, and other less obvious ones like icons. While the text is also a component of a layout design and, in many ways, inseparable from visual objects, this Step will mostly focus on presenting imagery. Visual design elements aim to build a well-organized, dynamic composition that provides information quickly and clearly while keeping the audience engaged.

DON'T forget:
good composition
is often about
simplifying.

Once you determine the structure of your grid, you then begin to pay close attention to your content objects and all the design details of a layout. Whether you are creating a physical, digital or website portfolio, the visual principles listed below are central tools to achieving a successful and effective design, regardless of the medium:

proximity •
alignment and spacing •
scale and proportion •
color •
hierarchy •
visual balance •
similarity •

Although these visual design principles are often considered the standards to follow, they are, as with grid systems, not hard and fast regulations. Rather than relying solely on these principles, you also need to use your own intuition, logic and visual skills to create a balanced and visually appealing layout. Just remember, the aim is to present your content in a layout that is clear and expressive. On the other hand, a carelessly constructed layout can result in an ineffective or negative experience for the viewer, regardless of how excellent your projects may be. Therefore, though you need not be ruled by these visual principles, understand them as guides that will help you develop a layout that effectively connects you to your audience.

PROXIMITY —

WHY PAY ATTENTION TO PROXIMITY

When designing a layout, it's pivotal to first consider the concept of proximity. This refers to the visual relationship between different objects in a composition. Proximity works intuitively. If images and text are placed close to each other, it indicates that they have equal importance or are related in some way. Conversely, if they are separated, it implies that they are unrelated and are being kept apart by strategically using negative space. Thus, when applying the principle of proximity to your layout, you should consider all the individual objects and their relationships to one another. By identifying those connections you can, for instance, arrange related objects near each other or set apart images with different messages. Then, your layout will provide a clear order and intuitive comprehension, making it easier for viewers to understand and navigate through the design.

— ALIGNMENT AND SPACING

DO place an content object slightly out of alignment. It will make it stand out.

Alignment /as well as spacing / is another significant design principle that is only subtlety visible, which may be why it is often undermined and easily neglected. The truth is that misalignment or improper spacing is what usually catches the eye, which is why it so critical. Although alignment is often associated with text formatting, it is equally important in organizing your other content objects. Alignment creates spatial relationships in layout and emphasizes meaning or visual connection by positioning related objects on the same axis of established grid lines. Conversely, intentional misalignment of an object that is part of a larger, perfectly aligned group can create tension and draw attention to the offset or isolated object, effectively bringing a visual order and interest to the composition. However, it's important to use this technique judiciously, as the lack of alignment or misalignment without a purpose can result in a disorganized message and lack of cohesiveness in the overall design. When done correctly, alignment orders your layout design, guiding the viewer's eye through the content and reinforcing the overall hierarchy. An important, perhaps obvious note is that alignment occurs both horizontally and vertically, so both should be considered when designing.

Spacing is the deliberate, strategic arrangement of gaps between your objects. Effective spacing requires you to consider proportions in the spacing between objects, such as large images or, if designing a website, small buttons. When done right, it can reinforce clarity, functionality and overall perception of your composition. On the other hand, inadequate

VISUAL PRINCIPLES

proximity

  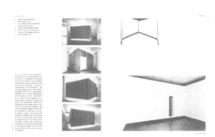

ELIZABETH ADEBAYO   PAIGE DAVIDSON

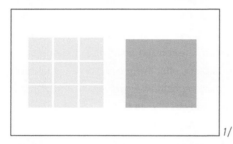

1/

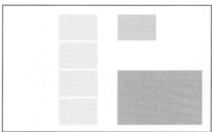

2/

1/ The physical proximity of objects placed next to each other suggests they are part of the same message.
2/ Separated objects appear to indicate different ideas.

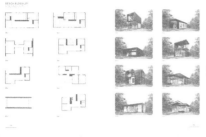

alignment

ROBERTO VARGAS   JEK KEE LIM

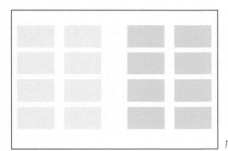

1/

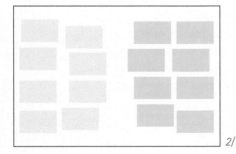

2/

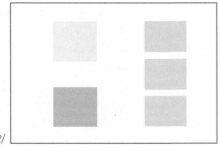

1/ Strictly aligned multiple objects that come together as a single entity create harmony and unification.
2/ Lack of alignment disconnects their meaning and conceals intention.

1/ A misaligned object becomes more noticeable. This interruption could be desirable if the object needs more attention.
2/ An obeyed alignment creates the perception of a unified message.

spacing can make your objects appear crowded, posing challenges for viewers to differentiate between various objects. Poor spacing is more than just poor aesthetics — it disturbs the practical function of your layout.

SCALE AND PROPORTION —

WHY SCALE
MATTERS

Scale and proportion are two fundamental concepts that are related to size, but they have distinct meanings. In portfolio design, scale refers to the relative size of one object compared to other objects within a composition or compared to an overall reference point, such as the format size. One of the most significant effects of scale is the ability to create a sense of hierarchy and emphasis. For instance, larger objects are perceived as more important, while smaller ones feel subdued. This aspect of scale begins to deal with proportions as well as other visual principles like hierarchy, discussed later in this Step. However, it is important to first understand some of the effects of scale. When adjusting the scale of your content, be mindful that when objects become too small, this leads to a loss of detailed visual information. On the other hand, enlarging a content object beyond its original dimensions can result in a fuzzy or pixelated quality. Therefore, pay attention to the effects of scale, not only in terms of hierarchy but also in terms of clarity. Always run a quick test to ensure your line weights deliver desirable clarity, especially when modifying the scale of technical drawings containing line weights, hatches, and text labels. By being attentive to the effects of scale, you can use it effectively as another tool for your design layout.

DON'T stretch your imagery out of proportion. Avoid distortions.

DO test print your drawings to see if you need to re-scale line weights to ensure clarity for a print copy.

*DO remember that
equal proportions
create monotony.*

While proportion relates to the size of objects, it's more accurate to say that, proportion is the relationship between objects and how their size, visual weight, and quantity interact with one another in an overall composition. An effectively proportioned layout requires establishing harmony in the size and impact of objects, but sometimes also a meaningful differentiation.

To achieve a well-proportioned layout, you should start by placing objects with common features together. Using consistent spacing and scale for these objects will create a sense of unity in your layout. Additionally, then, to break up the drab monotony of identical objects, consider, for instance, creating major and minor zones within the layout using varying scales and spacing. Such a method adds interest and a sense of hierarchy. Be sensible and keep a balance, though, and avoid significant differences that can make objects appear unrelated, disordered or overshadowed. A poorly proportioned layout can confuse and disengage the audience.

— COLOR

The use of color in layout design should be done with intention and purpose. Although colors can create a desired mood or serve as a graphic detail, they should not be relied upon to compensate for a lack of visual content or excitement in a portfolio. Reflecting your personality in your portfolio should be a part of your design process, but be mindful that the color should spring naturally from the content in your portfolio.

VISUAL PRINCIPLES

proportion

ALI ISMAIL KARIMI   ELISSA SUDARGO

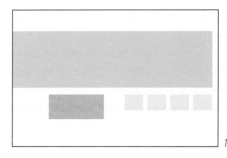

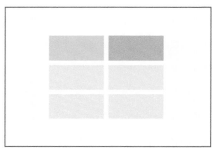

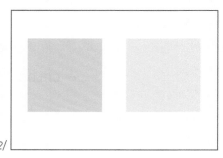

*1/ Different proportions and varied
scales or spacing contribute to an
informational order.
2/ Objects of the same scale are
viewed as a single entity.*

*1/ Different proportions of objects
create emphasis and order.
2/ Equal proportions lack focus and
may quickly disengage attention.*

color

CSENGE KIRÁLY

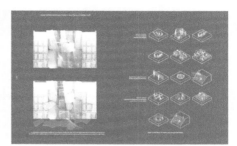

THIAGO LEE

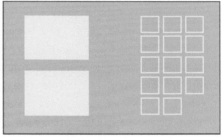

1/ The darker background color highlights light imagery, giving it strength against the full bleed on the right page.
2/ Eliminating the background contrast on the left causes the full bleed on the right to stand out.

1/ A solid dark background acts heavier than a light one. The dark elevates light objects.
2/ Removing the background color will reduce the weight of the objects.

Color can be presented in several ways within a layout:

• full color in content objects – imagery
• solid color pages – section dividers, for instance
• color in textual elements

Typically color in layout is applied for hierarchy purposes, discussed more fully in the next section. Other than the color embedded in your content, using too much color without careful consideration can distract and detract from your work. To maintain a professional approach, it might be best to stick to neutral color schemes with white or light-gray backgrounds. These backgrounds are clean and effective and enhance all types of imagery in your portfolio.

If you desire to use a color in your background to express the visual identity of your portfolio, you must let the tone exist as a supportive element that highlights your work. Many colors can be overpowering, but there are ways, if considered carefully, to create a fresh look with successful results. For example, applying a light tone of color that complements your imagery across an entire page can enhance the imagery. Or, another example, a layout with a full-bleed black background may create a strong impression providing a sharp contrast of solid color behind your content.

Another method to intensify your background color is through the use of gradient. Using gradients, however, requires a clear understanding and careful application. If you are not confident about your visual instincts or don't have experience applying multiple colors along with content, it's best to avoid using gradients altogether. On the other hand, when used correctly, a gradient background or partial application can add depth to your layout. Keep in mind that gradients are better suited for website portfolios rather than print copies. The online medium provides a wider range of colors and vivid looks on

DON'T use textures and patterns as a background for text. It may make your content hard to read.

a screen. Additionally, a website gives the possibility to scroll, so a gradient background can change as you move, creating a dynamic feel. When printing a gradient on physical paper, the colors may appear dull and have an unappealing banding effect, depending on the printer's quality.

— HIERARCHY

WHY IS VISUAL
HIERARCHY ESSENTIAL

DON'T neglect a visual hierarchy. Without it you appear to lack an understanding of your own work.

Although this visual principle was introduced with the grid system and already referred to throughout this Step, the vital importance of hierarchy in layout design requires that it be emphasized again. Even the most captivating layout can be confusing if viewers cannot navigate it, do not know where to focus, or cannot identify the most significant objects. In other words, without a clear visual hierarchy, your best designs could be easily overlooked. If you execute your visual hierarchy properly, you will ease your viewers' navigation and enhance their appreciation not only of your layout composition but of your content — the work itself!

DO remember that hierarchy is your power tool!

Once again, to establish a hierarchy, determine which content objects are most important and should be seen first. These primary objects should be followed by secondary and tertiary objects. Then, the methods and tools discussed earlier and listed below should be used to differentiate and order the objects so that viewers can quickly understand their importance and flow:

scale •
color and contrast •
white space •
proximity •
alignment •

VISUAL BALANCE —

WHY VISUAL
BALANCE MATTERS

Visual balance is one of the most important visual principles of composition and visual communication. The purpose of visual balance in portfolio design is to distribute visual weight evenly across your layout. Visual weight is understood as the amount of attention that a viewer gives to a single object in your composition. Every object used in your design, all the graphics and text, carries a certain visual weight. Altogether, the content objects work as a unified whole, deploying a balanced design that naturally pleases the eye and manifests a sense of comfort, harmony and equity. However, this doesn't mean that the visual weight of your objects has to be equal to each other to achieve a visual balance, nor should a sense of hierarchy be abandoned. Rather, it means that no objects should be too dominant or too subordinate. A balanced layout design ensures that all objects of your composition get the proper attention from your audience.

Visual balance in composition can be achieved in many ways but there are only two main strategies:

- **symmetrical**
- **asymmetrical**

Symmetrical balance is a design technique in which the content objects are mirrored or evenly arranged on both sides of a central axis. This creates a sense of balance as the visual weight of the objects on either side is the same. Such an equal set of arrangements typically feels subconsciously pleasing because it looks organized, and stable. For instance, if you have visually similar or equally important objects in your layout and you don't want them to compete, it's best to opt for a symmetrical arrangement. However, because

DO avoid using absolute symmetry in every single layout. It encourages scanning.

DO rest your eyes periodically throughout the day. You will see better.

of its static, predictable, and somewhat simple nature, a symmetrical layout can cause viewers to quickly resolve your content and begin scanning, leading to disengagement and lack of attention.

DO consider distributing white space asymmetrically to achieve a dynamic imbalance.

Asymmetrical balance, on the other hand, entails the uneven distribution of visual weight on either side of a central axis while still maintaining a sense of balance. This can be accomplished by varying an object's scale or strategic position, for instance, or by setting off a large object with several smaller ones. Because of the greater complexity of its unequal distribution, the asymmetrical balance demands more viewer attention as they process the varied relationships between the objects. If you want to draw a focus to a particular object in your composition or to inject more energy into your overall layout, you should strive to create an intentional imbalance. However, to successfully execute an asymmetrical composition, you need to first carefully consider the message you want to convey and then manipulate the placement and visual weight of your objects accordingly until the design is purposefully imbalanced. If you push too far, the distributed tension in your composition can create unwanted discomfort – a sense of being out of balance. When executed well, an asymmetric layout can result in a striking and captivating approach, as it deviates from the expected and captures the viewer's attention more effectively than perfectly balanced designs.

HOW TO ACHIEVE
A VISUAL BALANCE

Because an object's visual weight derives from many attributes there is no precise way to measure it. So, achieving a visual balance requires a strong visual sensibility and intuition. Below are some attributes that can be usefully manipulated, and then observations on how to effectively use each one:

• balance from scale
• balance from color
• balance from position

HOW TO ACHIEVE A VISUAL
BALANCE FROM SCALE

To achieve balance in the layout, one of the most common tactics is to adjust the scale of objects. There are two different methods to accomplish this, and each method produces a different effect. The first and most straightforward method is to use objects of equal size. This approach will create a symmetrical look that creates an orderly and aesthetically pleasing layout that is easy to decode and comprehend.

However, there is another more dynamic approach that can be equally or even more effective. This method involves using objects of different scales, which can generate a more energetic and engaging atmosphere for your layout. When using this method, you need to realize that larger objects carry more visual weight. To counterbalance that, you can simply group smaller objects to offset a large one. Or you can vary the scale of objects in your composition but then use other attributes, such as color, to achieve balance. Despite their different scales, objects can still feel visually equal.

HOW TO ACHIEVE A VISUAL
BALANCE FROM COLOR

All colors have a visual weight, but some carry more weight than others. This means that certain colors will matter more within an overall color combination. To adjust the visual balance of objects in your composition, you can affect the weight of each object by adjusting its color through these three components:

DO remember that warmer colors are heavier than cooler ones.

142

hue •
saturation •
value •

Pairing images with similar, analogous hues together can create a sense of balance and harmony. /Analogous hues are colors next to or near each other on the color wheel/. This balance could involve using greens and yellows or blue and green imagery, for instance. On the other hand, if you place next to each other images with contrasting, complementary hues /colors that are opposite each other on the color wheel/, the image with the darker hue would feel heavier than the image with a brighter hue. This effect produces an asymmetrical color balance, adding a more stimulating dynamic.

DO maintain consistent color modes across different softwares when editing an image.

Another factor to consider is saturation, which refers to the intensity of a color. Generally, high saturated images, which appear vivid, tend to attract more attention than those with low saturation and a faded look. In this context, it's important to ensure that the saturated image doesn't dominate the entire focus of the layout. To engage multiple saturated images in balance, consider using images of a complementary palette to equalize the visual weight.

Finally, the most decisive aspect in achieving color balance lies in manipulating value, which essentially represents the contrast between light and dark within an object. Objects with a darker shade and bolder contrast inherently carry a greater visual weight. With color imagery specifically, value is the most important factor as it determines how light or dark your image appears. Altering an image's color value can significantly impact its visual weight. To harmonize two images with, for instance, dissimilar hues or saturations, you can darken the contrast value of the weaker image to give it

VISUAL PRINCIPLES

hierarchy

NICHOLAS MACINTYRE   ABDAL KARIM RABI

1/

2/

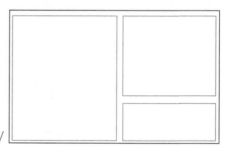

1/ A variety of object scales can reinforce the focus and order within a composition.
2/ A uniformity will equalize the importance of all objects.

1/ Darker color and higher contrast draws more attention.
2/ A monotone appearance lacks emphasis and direction.

visual balance

LUCIA KRIVÁ

ALI ISMAIL KARIMI

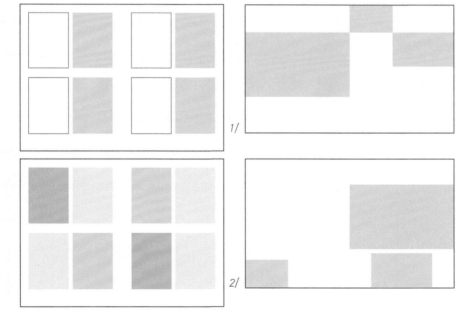

1/

2/

1/ Darker color objects placed with lighter ones create harmony and a natural emphasis.
2/ A lack of color balance appears overwhelming and lacks clear focus.

1/ An asymmetric composition places different visual weights on either side, without abandoning a sense of balance and visual order.
2/ Out of balance compositions lack a sense of purpose and flow.

more weight and attention. In another case, though, you may want similar values for images with different hues so that the deeper hue has weight and gains attention.

An additional note should be made about contrast. Colors with values that are too close to each other, in other words with a low contrast, appear flat and lack appeal. Effective use of contrast not only highlights important objects but also adds depth and dimension to the composition, making it visually stimulating and more compelling.

However, using contrast is essential not only when combining multiple images in a single composition but also within your content objects. If your image, drawing, or text appears faded and lacks distinctiveness, the viewer may struggle to perceive the information or message you are trying to convey. Therefore, you may need to adjust the saturation, hue, contrast and brightness of the imagery in photo editing software like Adobe Photoshop or GIMP. However, it's important to be careful not to go overboard, as excessive adjustments can make your work appear unnatural or misrepresented. If you are unsure about the contrast manipulations, try testing your image in gray-scale tones first. This essentially strips down the hue and saturation from your image to reveal the blandness or intensity of your image color values. If your image in a monochrome rendition feels bland, that's when you should adjust the intensify some color attributes.

DO use different contrast values to shift or attract the viewer's focus.

HOW TO ACHIEVE A VISUAL BALANCE FROM POSITION

Another way to achieve balance in your layout composition is to pay attention to the positioning of your content objects. This principle is primarily based on the proportion, proximity, and quantity of objects within the composition. One simple way to achieve a visually balanced composition is by having equally sized objects placed on the same grid lines on both

DO keep in mind that vertical objects appear heavier than horizontal ones.

sides of an axis. However, a more expressive and imbalanced arrangement can be created by intentionally placing an object off-center from the central axis grid. In another scenario, if some of your objects are positioned higher in the layout or placed further from the dominant area or object in your composition, they tend to become visually heavier and, therefore, more balanced compared to those positioned lower or more compactly. Lastly, objects placed on the right side of a spread will likely feel heavier than those on the left.

Also, if you are dealing with asymmetry in your layout, such as from color imbalance, it's often best to use a sense of gravity when placing objects in your composition and letting heavy objects sink down, and lighter ones float up. That is, place your more weighted content objects at the bottom of your layout and lighter ones at the top.

— SIMILARITY

WHY USE
SIMILARITY

DON'T use disjointed graphic elements with differing styles or colors.

Creating a sense of continuity and cohesiveness without duplicating your content objects is the essence of similarity. It provides a basis and reference point that holds together disparate objects and creates cohesion without relying on symmetry, proximity or alignment. When you implement similarity, viewers easily recognize patterns and concepts throughout a larger body of your work, making it easier to understand and engage with the content. Similarity can be achieved in various ways, such as employing image crossovers in each of your project intro pages. You can also color code the backgrounds for each project to break the monotony but yet maintain coherency across the portfolio. Likewise, giving specific website buttons a consistent color

VISUAL PRINCIPLES

similarity

Design Lab
Platforms

Le Musée Imaginaire
the Museum for the Postdigital Age

BURAK CELIK

1/ A cohesive pattern established throughout project introductions enhances clarity and encourages easy navigation.
2/ Uncoordinated introductions upset a sense of pace and confuse navigation and the message.

similarity

ANASTASIIA PEROVA

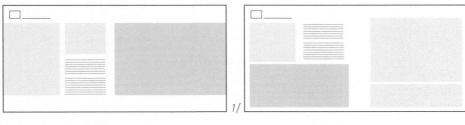

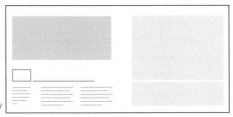

1/

2/

1/ Essential objects on the project introductions should remain consistent for a clear continuity. Some anomalies can create rhythm and interest.
2/ Introductions that break their pattern too much cause uncertainty and muddle your message.

can help users quickly and easily understand their purpose. Essentially, you can bring together objects through similarity and create a unified design that pleases the eye and facilitates the reader's experience.

However, it's important to note that sometimes breaking the pattern, even momentarily, can be just as effective, especially when you want to draw attention to a specific point or object. This can include using anomalies such as full-bleed images or implementing a free-style grid in a layout to create a sense of surprise that engages your audience. However, use these treatments with a well-considered strategy, as overuse can lead to confusion and subvert the purpose of similarity.

COMMON MISTAKES —

LACK OF
IMAGE CONTRAST

Even if your images are otherwise of the best quality, weakly defined contrast can significantly reduce the visibility and overall clarity, and impede viewer comprehension /see common mistakes 1/. While it is relatively easy to recognize proper contrast value in gray-scale imagery, it may be rather challenging with color images. However, you can evaluate the contrast of your images quickly and effectively by converting them to gray scale using any photo editing software. If your image in a gray scale feels bland, it signals the need to enhance contrast and perhaps also adjust saturation or hue to enliven the color image.

DO convert your image into gray scale to understand its true contrast.

Contrast holds double significance when working with line drawings, particularly when you adjust their scale /see common mistakes 2/. Your line drawings should be clear and distinguishable regardless of their size. To achieve clarity,

150

you may need to manually alter the scale of the line weights and hatches to ensure the information is accurate and easy to discern.

DO let the negative space become part of your layout. It will boost the clarity of your work.

Maintaining visual balance in a layout can contribute to a harmonious design and highlight specific objects. Neglecting balance can lead to a visually overwhelming and discomforting experience, making it difficult for the viewer to focus on particular objects or key information. This issue often arises when layouts contain too much intense and colorful imagery throughout the entire layout /see common mistakes 3/. In such compositions, your best work will most likely be lost or overlooked, compromising the intended message or purpose of your layout. To overcome this issue, try to counterbalance vivid imagery with lighter-weight imagery or by integrating negative space into your design. This will provide a visual relief and prevent an overly saturated feel.

Purposeful and deliberate imbalance in composition can bring a visually striking effect and dynamic quality to your layout as it disrupts expectations. However, achieving a compelling imbalanced equilibrium requires a trained eye, whether it be yours or someone else's. Weak execution or unintentional neglect of visual balance can fail to capture the viewer's attention effectively. This often occurs when parts of your layout become cluttered or visually heavy, while others remain oddly sparse with randomly arranged objects without a clear purpose or level of prominence. This could also be caused by poorly managed negative space in a layout or when images of significantly different visual weights are placed in close proximity /see common mistakes 4/. Weakly executed equilibrium will discourage a proper attention to your objects. Therefore, to successfully integrate a visual imbalance into your layout, experiment with different asymmetrical arrangements until they achieve the required purpose, flow and level of attention for all of the objects used in your composition.

LACK OF
VISUAL HIERARCHY

Remember, you may only have a brief time to convey the message of your portfolio. To make sure the attention you desire is achieved quickly, apply one of the most powerful tools you have available — hierarchy. If you don't carefully consider the order in which you present information and assign importance to each object, your portfolio can end up being either too dull or too chaotic. This can leave your viewer struggling to identify the most important information, and they may quickly lose interest in your portfolio /see common mistakes 5, 6/. Use the visual principles discussed in this Step to create a visual hierarchy that makes your portfolio easier to navigate as well as captivating. A portfolio that achieves your goals!

DO identify the "star" images of every single project and highlight them prominently.

IMPROPER
SCALING

When scaling down an image, always ensure that the message and information included in it are still easy to discern. This is especially critical when it comes to technical drawings. Scaling down a set of drawings to fit a page can be problematic when they contain line weights, hatches and text labels /see common mistakes 7/. If you are printing your portfolio, always run a quick test to make sure that your line weights are clear and your image delivers the desired quality. No matter your medium, if the image is too small, it won't be able to show off the effort that you have put into it. Beyond that, your image can be misinterpreted if you don't prioritize clarity during the scaling process.

DO keep in mind that scaling drawings that contain hatches can cause the hatch to become too sparse or dense.

Also, remember that oversizing your content objects might also have negative consequences as it may obscure information. Oversized, cramped compositions cause viewers to struggle to see where they should focus their attention /see common mistakes 8/. By carefully considering the size and placement of objects, you can create a design that not only pleases a professional's eye but speaks in a clear language.

INCONSISTENCY
THROUGH THE PORTFOLIO

Consistency is an overarching quality that is inherent to architecture but also to product design, graphic design, user-experience design and other aesthetic fields. And consistency should be maintained throughout your portfolio design as well. It provides the aesthetic value of unity and the functional purpose of ease of use. Similarity, the like appearance of objects, discussed in this Step, is one aspect of consistency.

Inconsistency works against you, as it draws viewers' attention to the oddities in your compositions rather than the content of your work /see common mistakes 9,10/. Remember that the human eye can very easily recognize patterns and consistency, and even an untrained eye quickly notices errors and irregularities. It might be hard to trick an architect's eye!

COMMON MISTAKES

contrast

1/

2/

1/ *Lack of contrast in the image can make details indistinct and cloud your intended message.*

2/ *Line drawings on a dark background may lead to reduced clarity, and visual fatigue.*

Achieving an adequate contrast requires you to carefully consider color choices along with making necessary adjustments to brightness and contrast settings so that all your content stands out distinctly.

IMAGES THIS PAGE BY TREVOR RODGERS

visual balance

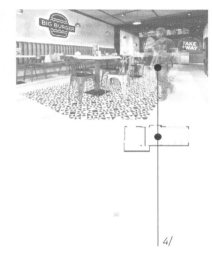

3/

4/

3/ *If all objects within a composition are boldly colored, they will compete for attention and none will stand out.*

4/ *A poor balance of visual weight can lead to an awkward composition. Disoriented viewers may leave some of the content unnoticed.*

Creating intentional imbalance can be a powerful design choice, but make sure to do it with a clear purpose. Consider the colors, scale, placement and proper distribution of weights to achieve a visually appealing and well-balanced design.

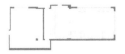

IMAGES THIS PAGE BY LUCIA KRIVÁ

COMMON MISTAKES

hierarchy

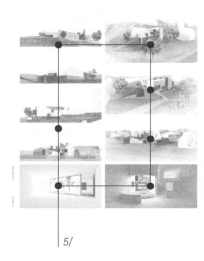

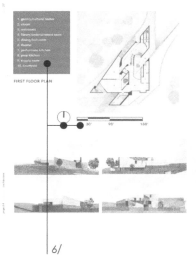

5/

6/

5/ Equal visual weights distributed across the layout create uncertainty in the priority of information.

6/ Improper visual hierarchy creates dissonance, with less pertinent objects overshadowing more essential ones.

Always give thoughtful attention to visual hierarchy. Ensure that the overall visual weights of your images /scale, position, contrast, color, etc./ align with your priorities and intentions for the content.

scale

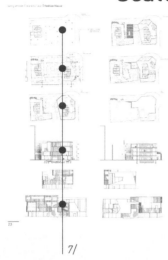

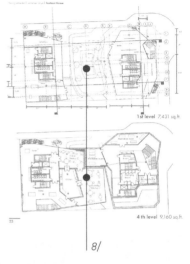

7/

8/

7/ *Drawings that are too small become illegible and provide no useful information.*

8/ *Large drawings can overwhelm a layout and crowd out perceptions.*

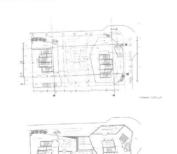

Make drawings and other imagery approachable, comfortably spaced with information that is clearly decipherable. Reduce the number of objects on in a layout to prevent overcrowding. Relocate objects, or remove them altogether if necessary.

IMAGES THIS PAGE BY LUCAS DENMEADE

COMMON MISTAKES

inconsistency

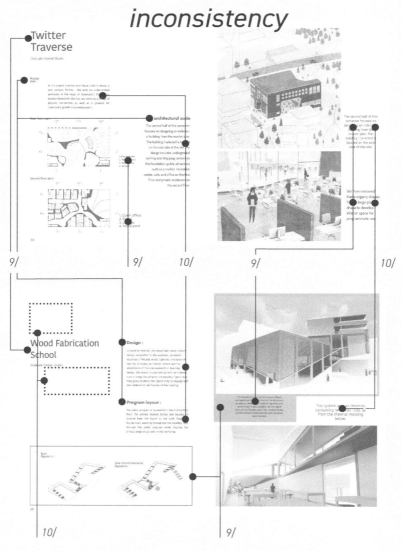

9/ *Lack of a consistent visual theme, including fonts and other graphics, can make a portfolio look disjointed and the content seem haphazard.*

10/ *Varying paragraph widths or alignments disrupts related information. Irregular placements within project introductions make navigation difficult.*

Twitter
Traverse

Graduate Context Studio

Master
plan :

In this project, I worked with Devin Gallo to design a new campus facility. We took an underutilized peninsula in the heart of Cendaruti's three main popular downtown districts and serves as a bridge of physical connection as well as a grounds for community growth and development.

Architectural
scale :

Any foreign includes underground parking and shopping centers on the foundation, public attractions such as a market, restaurant center, cafe, and office on the first floor and private resident use on the second floor.

First floor
plan :

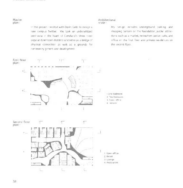

Core tradeline
2 Two bedrooms
3 Open office
4 Terrace

Second floor
plan :

1 Open office
2 Retail
3 Lounge
4 Restaurant

30

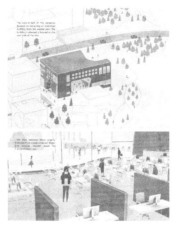

IMAGES IN UPPER SPREAD BY EVAN BLUEMEL

Wood
Fabrication
School

Graduate Context Studio

Design :

Located in Indonesia, the Wood Fabrication School brings recognition to the essential, abundant material of Vincent wood right into the heart of the city. Focusing on Finnish culture and the importance of the core elements in building design, the school is planned out with an indoor/semi strategy focusing on the meaning figural structure that gives students the opportunity to engage with the outdoors or utilization of the building.

Program
layout :

The entire program is located from the first to third floor. The private student library and housing is located from the fourth to the sixth floor. The figural icon moving throughout the building cuts through the public program while shaping the private program as seen in the structure.

Stair
figuration :

Stair interior/exterior
figuration :

The sidewalk acts as freedom contradicts head that does as from the freedom moving debate.

30

IMAGES IN LOWER SPREADS BY EMILY USSIA

To create comprehensive yet quickly-identifiable content within a layout, you should make all the related groups consistent, including fonts and paragraph widths and alignments. To reinforce a clear navigation, maintain the same placement of paragraphs in each section introduction.

STEP 7

— LAYOUT
TEXTUAL ELEMENTS

Textual layout elements are the final components of your portfolio's visual communication design. Your text ought to speak in the most direct, clear way to complete the full message of your portfolio. These elements deliver a written message, of course, but they are still visual elements within the layout, and it is typography that makes all the textual elements understandable and visually appealing. Although a reader's very first reaction to textual elements may be subtle and subconscious, you still must take the role of your text and its appearance seriously. This Step will apply some visual principles introduced in earlier Steps as they help you to understand how textual elements cohere within an overall design.

— TYPOGRAPHY

WHAT DOES
TYPOGRAPHY INVOLVE

Typography is the art of arranging and presenting text in a visually compelling and clear manner. Typography arranges individual letters as well as large fields of text, and makes use of an array of typefaces, fonts and many spacing variables such as leading. In portfolio design, your typography should deliver clear language in an easily read way, but also continue to communicate the message that you have shaped with your imagery. The text in a portfolio layout primarily includes these distinct components:

heading / project title •
subheading / project details •
body text / project description •
caption / image description •
folio / page number •

Each of the text components has its own role and importance, and as such, each component has its own visual style. At the same time, however, each must cohere to an overall style. Headings are meant to capture the attention of the audience with their eye-catching typography, whereas body text and captions provide more descriptive and supportive information with easy-to-read typography. At a subordinate level, but still important, are the folio and other navigation components discussed in Step 8. Their purpose is to guide the viewer through the document with easy-to-find lettering. Since each text component contributes to effective communication, be sure each fulfills its role clearly and adds to the visual experience.

DO remember that fonts are not just an aesthetic decision. They have a function.

WHAT IS
TYPEFACE AND FONT

Typography uses typefaces to create readable and stylistically compelling text. Typefaces, also known as font families, offer you a wide array of design possibilities, with each typeface having unique features that remain consistent across all characters and sizes of text. This is where fonts themselves come in. There is a widespread misconception that font and typeface are interchangeable terms. In reality, fonts are not typefaces. Typefaces are the design style of characters with a consistent visual appearance, such as Arial, Helvetica, and Futura. A font, on the other hand, refers to individual stylistic variations within a typeface, like its size and weight. An example of font could be Helvetica, 9 pt, Regular or Futura, 15.5 pt, Light Italic.

When it comes time to determine the look of your text, you will have two decisions to make. The typeface is a fundamental decision that shapes the overall visual impression of both the text and the portfolio itself. Then, font selection within a typeface also significantly contributes to the visual impact.

Choosing the wrong typeface as well as the font can make the text challenging to read and even distort its meaning, ultimately disconnecting your audience from your message. You need to invest time and effort into carefully selecting the typeface and font that complements your content.

— TYPEFACE SELECTION

WHAT ARE THE CATEGORIES OF TYPOGRAPHY

Prior to choosing a specific typeface, first narrow down your choices by familiarizing yourself with the four primary style categories of typography: Serif, Sans Serif, Script /also known as handwriting/, and Display /also known as decorative/. Among these styles, Serif and Sans Serif are the most commonly used and are appropriate for print and screen use. Script and Display typefaces are probably not ideal for a portfolio as they can convey an unprofessional impression and be more difficult to read. Therefore, avoid using those categories of typeface and instead, opt for Serif or Sans Serif to achieve a more dignified look and an easier reading experience.

HOW TO BEGIN TYPEFACE SELECTION

Choosing the right typeface is a blend of solid principles and intuitive judgment, and it can require years of experience to develop a good sense of it. Though there are no hard and fast regulations on how to choose the perfect typeface, there are some guides that can make the process simpler.

TYPE CLASSIFICATIONS

The studio was filled with the rich odor of roses, and when the light summer wind stirred amidst the trees of the garden, there came through the open door the heavy scent of the lilac.

serif

Serif type is quickly distinguished and encourages flow across a line, especially in long texts of smaller font.

The studio was filled with the rich odor of roses, and when the light summer wind stirred amidst the trees of the garden, there came through the open door the heavy scent of the lilac.

sans-serif

Sans-serif type looks modern, clean and reads well on screens.

The studio was filled with the rich odor of roses, and when the light summer wind stirred amidst the trees of the garden, there came through the open door the heavy scent of the lilac.

script

Script type mimics hand-written letters. It can appear as too casual or even too formal, and almost always unprofessional.

The studio was filled with the rich odor of roses, and when the light summer wind stirred amidst the trees of the garden, there came through the open door the heavy scent of the lilac.

display

Display types are decorative in various attention-getting ways. Readability is not a priority, and their boldness can compete with imagery.

LEVELS OF TEXT HIERARCHY

title

20 pt bold
Suggests importance.
Feels strong, but perhaps
overpowering.

The studio was filled with the rich odor of roses, ...

body text

9 pt regular
Modest and legible.
Still easy to read.

The studio was filled with the rich odor of roses, and when the light summer wind stirred amidst the trees of the garden, there came through the open door the heavy scent of the lilac, or the more delicate perfume of the pink-flowering thorn.

captions

7 pt regular
Could become illegible,
especially for older readers.

The studio was filled with the rich odor of roses, and when the light summer wind stirred amidst the trees of the garden, there came through the open door the heavy scent of the lilac, or the more delicate perfume of the pink-flowering thorn.

One of the fundamental guidelines is to restrict the use of typefaces to two. But even pairing two different typefaces, which might be tempting in order to create a contrast and hierarchy, requires knowledge and a discerning eye. Many recommend choosing one serif and one sans-serif typeface to ensure contrast without clash; one typeface serves as the primary, while the other acts as the secondary or complementary typeface. However, it's not as straightforward as it sounds. Some serif and sans-serif combinations may create unintended tension due to stark differences. Therefore, if you're not well-versed in typography, it's best to avoid using multiple typefaces altogether, as such a design can lead to a chaotic and unprofessional appearance. A single typeface throughout a portfolio can bring order while still presenting a dynamic set of font styles and weights.

DO limit the typefaces in your document to no more than two.

WHAT ELSE TO CONSIDER IN TYPEFACE SELECTION

Your chosen typeface should harmonize with your portfolio style and content to reinforce your message. So, don't rely on widely used typefaces that are software defaults such as Myriad Pro, Times New Roman, or Arial. They are perfectly fine typefaces, but because of their overuse, they might not provide the uniqueness and distinctiveness your portfolio deserves. At the same time, don't go the other way too far and use a typeface that is overly stylized or merely focuses on expressing your personality. With typefaces, you need to strike a balance between a unique look with a sense of identity and the need for a typeface that is professional and has a more universal, functional appeal /see the discussion of legibility in the next section/.

DON'T pick a default software typeface. Show your attention to detail through a typeface that resonates with your work.

Navigating your typeface selection to find what complements your work and style can be a daunting task. The visual tone of your work, however, could be a key guide in this process.

For instance, if your work conveys minimalistic, lively, or even technical or unconventional vibes, a sans serif typeface may be a suitable choice to express your visual identity. On the other hand, if your representation suggests artistic, glamorous, sophisticated, or serious aesthetics, the serif typeface may be a better fit. If you are unsure or even lost in the type selection, there are some typefaces that usually work in any design project. Generally, Sans Serif typefaces like Futura, Proxima Nova, Open Sans, Roboto, Lato, or Europa are safe but respectable choices. For Serif typefaces, options like PT Serif, Georgia, Libre Baskerville, Merriweather, Alegreya, or Lora can work well and won't embarrass you.

While there are numerous websites where you can download from an ever-widening selection of fonts, not all of them offer high-quality options suitable for a project like a portfolio. For the best outcomes, use websites that guarantee the quality of their fonts, such as:

google fonts – free •
adobe fonts – paid •
creative market – free and paid •
font shop – paid •
dafont – free and paid •

Note, also, that if you're designing a website portfolio, make sure the fonts you choose are web-safe. This means that you'll need to choose a standard font that can be viewed on any device or operating system, or you will need to load font files directly to your site or provide a link to font files. Be sure to thoroughly test your font performance across browsers and platforms.

FORMATTING FOR READABILITY —

WHY AIM FOR LEGIBILITY AND READABILITY

A critical consideration for selecting an appropriate typeface is legibility. This means that you will want to use a typeface that is clear to the eye and quickly identifiable. A legible font doesn't compromise the distinctiveness of letters and allows for seamless reading. Beyond legibility, you must also consider the broader concept of readability, which measures how easy it is for the reader to understand the text, which can be significantly affected by the typeface, font variations, and formatting of text. A readable text resides in reducing the effort required to read and make sense of the text. Readability encourages your reader to read what you have to say. Below are typographical factors that can enhance readability:

DO remember that font legibility can differ when shifting between print and screen.

- font size and weight
- line spacing – leading
- line length
- font color and contrast
- text alignment

HOW TO PICK A FONT SIZE AND WEIGHT

One of the most significant factors that impact readability is the font size. Unfortunately, there is no one-size-fits-all formula for determining the perfect font size, as it varies depending on factors such as typeface style, the amount of text and the context. However, generally, a good reading font size for body text, which includes your brief paragraphs of project description, typically ranges between 9 pt and 11 pt. Some typefaces, like Open Sans or Helvetica, remain legible at 9 pt, but others, like Futura, become difficult to read at

DON'T oversize your fonts. They can distract focus from the imagery.

the same size. Captions and folios are usually even smaller than 9 pt, typically 7-8 pt. Anything smaller than this can be difficult to decipher.

As for a website portfolio, the most comfortable reading experience is achieved when the body text size ranges from 14 pixels to the more favorable 16 pixels. If the selected typeface has larger characters, you can comfortably work with 14 px, which is the minimum size recommended. Because your portfolio website is going to be viewed on mobile devices as well, you may want to adopt relative font size units for responsive design. For that use relative units, such as em, ex or rem, as opposed to absolute units such as px, or pt. There are online guides to units available, such as w3schools.com, where you can test out your font sizes and their readability.

DO remember, bolder fonts feel heavier so you may need to increase their leading.

Adjusting font weight /thickness/ is another way to improve text readability. A general guide is that the lighter or bolder your font weight is, the larger your font size must be to provide a comfortable reading experience. For instance, for body text it's usually best to use font weights that are "regular" or close to it since they have a more proportional stroke-to-space ratio.

HOW TO SET UP LINE SPACING

DO increase the leading for smaller text or long paragraphs for better readability.

Line spacing, or leading, refers to the space between the lines within a paragraph. If the spacing is too narrow or too loose, your text will become difficult to read. Although the leading depends on your selected typeface and font characteristics, generally speaking, you should go with 140–170% of your font size. For instance, if your font size is 9 pt, your line spacing should be at least $9 \times 1.4 = 12.6$ pt /140%/. This simple calculation ensures that the text is easy to read and doesn't feel cramped. The line spacing of the text you're reading has been set at 160%.

TEXT READABILITY

size and weight

THE PICTURE OF DORIAN GRAY

The studio was filled with the rich odor of roses, and when the light summer
wind stirred amidst the trees of the garden,...

leading

THE PICTURE OF DORIAN GRAY

The studio was filled with the rich odor of roses,
and when the light summer wind stirred amidst the
trees of the garden,...

line length

THE PICTURE OF DORIAN GRAY

The studio was filled with the rich odor of roses, and when the light summer wind stirred
amidst the trees of the garden, there came through the open door the heavy scent of the lilac.

contrast

THE PICTURE OF DORIAN GRAY

The studio was filled with the rich odor of roses, and
when the light summer wind stirred amidst the trees
of the garden,...

alignment

THE PICTURE OF DORIAN GRAY

The studio was filled with
the rich odor of roses, and when the light summer
wind stirred amidst the trees of the garden,...

*The block of text below is
a sample of well-formatted
readable text, with appropriate
leading, alignment, contrast and
line length.*

THE PICTURE OF DORIAN GRAY

The studio was filled with the rich odor of roses, and
when the light summer wind stirred amidst the trees of
the garden, there came through the open door the heavy
scent of the lilac.

HOW TO SET UP
LINE LENGTH

Keeping track of line length is a simple yet effective way to enhance readability. Excessively long lines can tire the reader's eyes and slow the line-to-line transitions, while lines that are too short can result in missed words, confusion and the need for re-reading. To keep the reader engaged, you should aim for an optimal line length of 50–75 characters. This text you're reading has an average of about 60 characters per line.

HOW TO SET TEXT
COLOR AND CONTRAST

Establishing high contrast is essential for enhancing text readability and especially accessibility. If there's not enough contrast between the text and the background color, it could strain the reader's eyes and cause them to miss out on important information. This can be particularly challenging for readers with impaired vision, those using low-quality screens, or anyone reading in bright sunlight. However, if the contrast is too extreme, such text can be jarring to look at and irritating to try to read. For example, using white text on a black background can appear fuzzy or even haloed. A similar effect can occur with text and background both set in complementary colors, like red text color set against a blue background or green text on a red background. Avoid such vibrant color combinations as they require frequent refocusing and visual discomfort, and instead, prioritize accessibility over your aesthetic preferences.

DO use black or at least darker tones for body text. Good contrast promotes readability.

To achieve optimal contrast, it's best to reserve applications of color for brief spans of text, such as titles, or components like buttons and links for a website portfolio. When it comes to body text, it might be best to stick to what's standard, particularly if the information in your paragraphs is important. Black, gray, or white on a high-contrast background will

DO ask others to read through your text. Does it read easily?

always work well for body text and will still allow you to create a strong sense of hierarchy. To make your portfolio accessible, especially important with a website, you should use an online tool such as color-blindness.com to ensure that the color combinations you have chosen for your text meet accessibility standards.

Finally, when adding text on top of an image, make sure that both the text and the image are clear and distinguishable. Otherwise, the text may blend into the image, making it difficult to read. To overcome this, you can either adjust the brightness of your image or place an opaque or semi-transparent object underneath your text to dim the image. This will help both the image and the text to stand out clearly.

HOW TO SET
TEXT ALIGNMENT

DON'T center longer texts. Jagged edges make the reading difficult.

Text alignment refers to arranging text so that it aligns within a larger composition. Alignment helps to organize the text to be easily readable and joins it into the overall layout. Most importantly, alignment guides the reader's eye through the textual content which significantly contributes to readability. Despite its importance, though, text alignment is often overlooked or haphazardly applied. So, pay attention to this mundane, seemingly invisible concept that plays a vital role in the effectiveness of a layout.

Different alignments are more suitable for different types of text when creating a layout. For example, paragraphs with a lot of text, such as body text, usually need left alignment with a defined left edge that's most comfortable for easy reading. This method gives the eye a clear and visible reference point to return to after reaching the end of each line. Then again, for languages that read from right to left, such as Arabic, right alignment should be used instead, for the same principle of accommodating natural reading flow. Centered and right-aligned text can be suitable for shorter texts, such as titles or captions, but it is not recommended for body text as it can unnecessarily create reading difficulties.

Another method which creates a clean and professional-looking paragraph is a justified alignment that aligns both the left and right edges. This forms straight margins on both sides, creating clear text blocks within your layout. However, you should be careful, as "full justification" can create uneven spacing between words, commonly known as "rivers," which can hinder readability. If the river gaps are too large, you can turn on a hyphenation option /which can also lead to poor readability/ or manually adjust the spaces between the words to eliminate the large gaps. If you prefer to use center-aligned text, keep the text short and with no more than five words per line to prevent difficulty and slower reading, as the reader always has to re-locate the start of the next line. Lastly, always remember that text alignment should be less of a stylistic choice but rather a design decision made with the user's best experience in mind.

DO avoid hyphen breaks in text blocks. It makes the text harder to read.

DESIGNING WITH TEXT —

WHAT IS A TEXT HIERARCHY

Organizing your textual content is just as important as organizing your visual content. Assigning your text to different levels of hierarchy will prioritize some information and create a seamless, well-ordered reading experience. A well-structured text hierarchy also serves as a powerful tool to narrate your projects, encouraging the reader to follow along and understand the progression of ideas and concepts as they move through your portfolio. When your textual content lacks order or appears randomly arranged, readers may struggle to discern the significance of each textual object, leading to quick scanning over your texts. Therefore, you should carefully structure your text hierarchy to direct your reader's attention and keep their engagement throughout their review of your work.

HOW TO ESTABLISH TEXT HIERARCHY

When establishing a text hierarchy, you should start by determining the number of levels you will have. While Step 8 thoroughly discusses what type information should be included, your portfolio layout design generally starts with at least these levels of hierarchy:

primary level – project title •
secondary level – project details •
tertiary level – project description •

DO test out your text hierarchy by staring at a space away from your actual design, and then looking back. What stands out first?

Once you determine all of your hierarchy levels, you should distinguish them based on their significance. The primary level is the most prominent text, whose role is to grab the audience's attention and point it toward other information. This is typically the title of your projects. In portfolio design the secondary and tertiary level are often close in hierarchy. The secondary level holds pivotal information, such as project details. This level shouldn't dominate like the first level, but it should be distinct enough to draw the reader's focus since it will provide them the essential aspects of the project. The tertiary level, then, is where you want your audience to arrive, perhaps even come to rest briefly. In a portfolio, this level represents your project description, the core of your textual content. Given its tertiary status, the font used shouldn't be overly emphasized, but it should prioritize readability.

175

Any additional information with lower importance, such as captions or folios, should receive the same or even lower emphasis yet remain visible and readable to clearly convey the necessary message.

HOW TO DESIGN
TEXT HIERARCHY

There are several attributes you can use to establish a clear and compelling text hierarchy. While experimenting with the following attributes you want to maintain a consistent and unified sensibility:

- **typeface**
- **font size**
- **font color and contrast**
- **alignment**
- **space and position**

HOW TO DESIGN
HIERARCHY WITH TYPEFACE

Using two different typefaces might initially seem like a good strategy to establish a text hierarchy. However, pairing typefaces can be challenging as your hierarchy can be easily ill-defined and less straightforward. A layout that uses a single typeface with no more than 3–4 different weights is a safer bet to create a professional and appealing design — safer than mixing typefaces. Therefore, when you're looking for a suitable typeface, look for one that offers at least the basic range of weight and slant options, such as Light, Light Italic, Regular, Italic, Bold, and Bold Italic. Some typeface families even provide a broader selection of font weights, ranging from Hairline or Extra Light to Black or Heavy styles. In certain instances, typeface families offer additional flexibility with options for width variations, such as extended and condensed styles. Regardless of the options you end up with, the point here is that having one typeface with a variety of font styles and weights allows for a more well-defined hierarchy.

DON'T use all caps for longer text. It makes your text difficult to read.

Because of their shared design characteristics, the variations within a typeface complement each other while being distinctly expressive. For example, a short line of text set in all-caps or upper-case font conveys focus and dominance, which is why it would be suitable for project titles. In other scenarios, setting information such as project details in italic style will distinguish it from the rest without adjusting size or color. On the other hand, the light or regular font weight carries less intensity, making it optimal for body text. By utilizing different font styles and weights within the same typeface, your layout will generate a hierarchy while maintaining a cohesive look — all without the difficulty of pairing different typefaces.

HOW TO DESIGN
HIERARCHY WITH FONT SIZE

DON'T set your size lower than 7 pt. It can become unreadable.

The most common and straightforward way to establish a hierarchy in the text is by using different font sizes. The larger the font, the greater importance it carries, which is why titles are typically set to a larger scale. While the size of the title is your design decision, keep in mind that it should be large enough to catch the reader's eye at the first moment but not so large that it overpowers the imagery. Text components such as body text or captions should be assigned with less priority and, therefore, set to a smaller font size. As body text is the meat among the text components, pay extra attention to find the optimal size that doesn't hinder the reading experience but also doesn't overwhelm the composition. Perhaps your body text should be established first, with other levels of text set in relation to the body text. Remember that while font size is a powerful tool for creating text hierarchy, it's not the only tool available. Consider other aspects to achieve an effective text hierarchy.

TEXT HIERARCHY EXAMPLES

Aa Bb

Different shades of the same font can be enough to achieve a distinctive text hierarchy.

Aa *Bb*

A hierarchy built on one typeface of different font styles can effectively distinguish the information.

CIUDAD COSTERA
Master Plan + Urban Design

The islet of San Juan faces a significant challenge: living up to its designation as a city. Being highly segmented, the urban design developed seeks to unify the neglected areas, encourage recreational pedestrian activity, highlight the quality of a coastal city, and create a town in a suburban place. The boardwalk, the strip that ties and connects the critical points of the city, is complemented by squares, viewpoints, promenades, parks intended for the enjoyment and use of pedestrians, and a boulevard that functions as the central pedestrian, vehicular, and visual connecting axis. In this exercise, we work with a large piece of land on the western end of the islet of San Juan. These lands are defined north and west by the Atlantic Ocean, south by the Luis Muñoz Rivera Park, and east by the Escambrón beach and the Caribe Hilton and Normandie hotels.

CLAUDIA CRESPO   ALI ISMAIL KARIMI

a**A** B b

*Different weights and sizes of
a single typeface separate the
multiple levels of hierarchy.*

A a B b

*A single font weight can establish
hierarchical order through the
use of varying sizes and spacing
between information groups.*

The site has an area of 340m2
and is located in a historical
neighborhood of Tehran. It
features sloped topography
and important vegetation that
requires to be preserved.

The Agricultural Shed; Redefined

The Great Plains, US

01

Slope House
Multi-Generational Housing

HOW TO DESIGN HIERARCHY
WITH FONT COLOR AND CONTRAST

Incorporating color into your text is an effective way to emphasize certain information without solely relying on font size. Subtle variations in shades of black, for instance, can already help establish a clear hierarchy. Also, brighter or contrasting colors can be particularly useful for making subordinate information, such as project descriptions, stand out while still keeping a title bold and prominent. In other instances, lighter shades of gray can be used for lower-level information, such as captions. Since captions are typically placed next to the imagery, a shade of gray still stands out without overpowering the image. However, as already emphasized, be careful when using lighter tones, since they can make the text hard to read against most backgrounds. Lastly, if you decide to use color to signify importance, make sure you use a consistent color scheme throughout your portfolio. Using too many colors in your text can quickly make your design feel visually noisy. Therefore, use the color strategically in your text, but do so with care and purpose.

DON'T underline text, especially body text. It creates visual noise and its purpose can be unclear.

HOW TO DESIGN TEXT
HIERARCHY WITH ALIGNMENT

Alignment is another attribute that can have a significant impact on the visual appeal of text and also on its hierarchal position. For instance, center-aligned text tends to appear dominant and can stand out, even without the use of other attributes such as font weight or color. Hence, center alignment is often employed for titles. On the other hand, left alignment, which is commonly used for body text, can provide a visually pleasing contrast and emphasis against higher-level information, as its jagged right side can break with blocky patterns. Full or right justification can be applied to text to set it apart from left-justified body text, providing alternative ways to create text hierarchy.

DON'T always attempt to align captions with body text. An offset caption can result in a more dynamic presentation.

HOW TO DESIGN TEXT HIERARCHY
WITH SPACE AND POSITION

DON'T locate the folio close to the inside margins, as its usefulness vanishes.

Once you've taken into account and implemented all the attributes mentioned above, you should then integrate space around and between your textual objects to reinforce your layout's order. In essence, spacing should be thought of as simply a visualization of relationships. This means that if your textual objects are assigned with adjacent levels of hierarchy, you should reduce the space between them to enhance their relationship. If they carry different meanings or levels of priority, increase space to distinguish them from one another. Or, if you deal with multiple textual objects of the same priority, you should balance their status by placing them together while maintaining enough space to visually separate them.

DO use white space to separate text of different hierarchy levels.

Besides spacing, the position of your textual objects within a composition can also enhance the text hierarchy. Perhaps, it's obvious that an important title prominently placed near the top of a layout naturally attracts the viewer's eye. However, it might be less realized that a block of text placed at the center of a layout also can be perceived as prominent, which is useful for highlighting key information. Unconventionally positioning primary content at the bottom can create visual intrigue but will still be perceived as secondary information. Such an approach could intentionally guide the viewer's eye down the page. Lastly, when laying out a spread of two pages, the right page is typically more dominant to the viewer making it an ideal place for your project introduction. This is especially true for physical materials.

COMMON MISTAKES —

POOR CHOICE OF
TYPEFACE AND FONT

One of the most prevalent issues in architectural portfolios is a poor choice of typeface and font. This problem can be evident in various ways, such as the excessive use of different typefaces, overly narrow or decorative typefaces, and even font sizes that are too small or large /see common mistakes 1,2, and 3/. These design flaws can make your portfolio look amateurish and noisy and, more importantly, can make it challenging for readers to decipher your project descriptions or navigate the website effectively. Since the typeface choice is central to the portfolio's communication, it is best to stick with only one typeface and approach font weights, sizes, and other attributes thoughtfully and purposefully to achieve your desired appearance and, especially, its functionality.

DO pay attention to text hyphenation, especially if you apply it to a longer text. Hyphenation slows reading.

UNCLEAR TEXT
HIERARCHY

A failure to establish hierarchy is one of the most frequent issues when working with text in a portfolio. This occurs when the same or very similar fonts are used for different levels of information. For instance, if both the title and body text share the same font size, and weight, it becomes challenging for readers to identify the main message of the layout /see common mistakes 4/. In another scenario, the text hierarchy may be present but not precisely correct, as it emphasizes information that shouldn't be of high priority, potentially leading to confusion and a misunderstanding of your message /see common mistakes 5/. This is why you need to create contrast and distinction between the different levels of text by using attributes described in this Step. However, it's equally important to not overemphasize text, as carelessly using fonts that are too large, bold, or overly colorful can detract from the aesthetics of your layout.

*DO remember,
your text must
make sense
and be easily
read to enhance
readability.*

While striving for an aesthetically pleasing layout, your primary focus should be on building aesthetics around functionality, ensuring that your text is readable. One frequently overlooked aspect is leading. Text that lacks sufficient space between lines can appear cramped, making it problematic to read /see common mistakes 6/. In such cases, readers may resort to scanning the text rather than engaging in a thorough read. A similar reaction happens if the leading is too loose, causing difficulties in connecting lines of text /see common mistakes 8/. To achieve adequate leading, refer to the leading calculations provided in this Step.

The functionality of your text also relies on appropriate alignment. While experimenting with different alignments is a good idea, keep in mind that centered or right-aligned paragraphs /in Western cultures/ as well as long lines of texts, can make longer passages difficult and tiring to read /see common mistakes 7 and 9/. Opting for shorter line lengths and employing appropriate alignments for longer texts will facilitate smooth eye movement through your text.

*DON'T place text
too close to layout
edges or other
objects.*

Lastly, keep in mind that text with a background or image underneath can be easily diluted and quickly turn off the reader's engagement with your text /see common mistakes 10/. Therefore, if you are placing text on top of a dark or vibrant color image or pattern, consider placing a white, semi-transparent block beneath it to ensure the text meets its function. However, if you do so, give a negative space or safe zone around your text to allow for a comforting reading experience /see common mistakes 11/.

COMMON MISTAKES

typeface

1/

2/

3/

1/ A poor combination of typefaces can bring a clash of typefaces.

2/ A condensed typeface makes content difficult to read.

3/ A good, legible typeface can become illegible in small point sizes.

To ensure readability, always consider a clean typeface with an appropriate font weight, size and leading. Let your text be read.

hierarchy

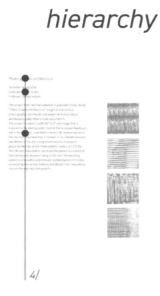

4/

5/

4/ *A text presented altogether in the same font size makes everything appear uniform. Nothing stands out.*

5/ *A hierarchy that is not established properly leads to confusing messages.*

To convey a coherent message, you must ensure that your hierarchy is set in a logical order at levels that are easily distinguishable from each other.

PHOTO-GRAPHIC ARCHITECTURE

Semester Spring 2023
Graduate Design Studio
Professor Deborah Azidyah

THIS PROJECT FROM MY FINAL SEMESTER IN GRADUATE SCHOOL, TITLED "PHOTO-GRAPHIC ARCHITECTURE," SOUGHT TO USE VARIOUS PHOTO-GRAPHIC TECHNIQUES AND EXPERIMENTS TO PRODUCE ARCHITECTURE, RATHER THAN SIMPLY DOCUMENT IT.

The project I created is a 30"x30"x1.5" site-image that is inspired by the photographs I took at the Goodyear headquarters in Akron, Ohio. I intended to create a 3D representation of the site and to achieve that, I zoomed in on different textures and details of the site. Using those textures, I created a grayscale bitmap, which then used to create a 3D STL file. This file was then used to carve out the pattern on a piece of hand-laminated plywood using a CNC mill. The resulting pattern is a beautiful and intricate representation of the site, discussing the various textures and details that I was able to capture through my photographs.

COMMON MISTAKES

readability

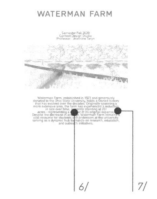

6/ Narrow leading blends lines together, making reading difficult.

7/ With centered alignment, it takes longer to locate the first word of the next line.

8/ Loose leading disconnects the lines, making reading challenging.

9/ Long lines are hard to follow as the transition from one line to next is slowed.

Whenever larger areas of text are involved, it's better to apply left or justified alignment. If you set the leading to at least 2.5 pt larger than the font size, your lines will be easier to follow.

IMAGES THIS PAGE BY EVAN BLUEMEL

readability

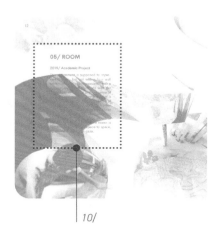

10/

11/

10/ Body text that is applied on top of a dark or intense color becomes illegible as it blends with it.

11/ A lack of marginal space around the text edges can feel cramped and negatively effect readability.

If you are placing text over an image, be sure it's readable. If not, use proper contrast and color, or a fill box placed beneath, so the text stands out and is legible.

STEP 8

COVER PAGE

RESUME

DESIGN STATEMENT

TABLE OF CONTENTS

INTRODUCTORY PROJECT PAGE

PROJECT PAGES

EXTRAS

THANK YOU AND
CONTACT INFORMATION

COMMON MISTAKES

— CONTENT
STRATEGY AND EXAMPLES

This guide has emphasized that your portfolio is a reflection of your professional identity, showcasing your character, passion, and design philosophy. You have already learned about the techniques that help you to prepare a functional, appealing layout. Now, it's time to compile all those layout principles while you incorporate all the necessary components of a portfolio. The aim of this Step is to review those components and the strategies to present them in the most effective and compelling way.

Although the components of the portfolio were introduced in Step 4, it will be helpful to list them out again to think more strategically about the appearance of each one:

cover page •
resume – optional •
design statement – optional •
table of contents •
introductory project page •
project pages •
extras – optional •
thank you and contact information •

COVER PAGE —

HOW TO START
WITH A COVER PAGE

When your audience receives your portfolio, it'll be your cover page they will look at first — not your impressive work inside. Just as you make your first snap judgments about a book based on its cover or, perhaps, a person based on their appearance, your cover page gives a first impression of you as a creative and critical thinker. It's a preview, or a visual cue of the design and content that is to follow. That said, your primary focus must be to grab attention quickly. Your audience will most likely have numerous other portfolios to review, so your cover must stand out. All this means you should be careful to leave enough time to give proper attention to designing your cover page. As you delve into designing your cover page, ask yourself these questions:

DO keep in mind that the cover page needs to show the essence of your portfolio.

- **What cover would grab my attention?**
- **What is my best skill?**
- **What do I want to convey about myself?**

WHAT ARE THE METHODS
FOR A COVER PAGE DESIGN

A cover page should delve beyond mere decoration; it should be grounded in intention, reflecting the essence of your work. This is an opportunity to showcase your creativity, sensibility, and identity in a single graphic statement. While this might feel exciting, it's equally challenging, as this task often ends with overly expressive designs that, in fact, obscure your individuality. The goal here is to keep the design compelling and captivating while maintaining clarity and focus so that your audience clearly understands the nature of your work and feels invited to explore your portfolio further. And here are several strategies to consider when designing your cover page:

DON'T include generic visuals for your cover or ones unrelated to your work. Choose an image that conveys your style.

imagery from the portfolio – models, visualizations... •
imagery that centers your ideas and intention – representation... •
graphic elements that show your sensibility – vectors or type •

In a portfolio website, the cover page translates as the site intro page — or homepage. A homepage acts as the first point of interaction when users open your link, which is very similar to the role of a standard cover page. Nevertheless, your tools to captivate the attention of your audience are now expanded, and so besides high-quality images, for example, you now have a chance to incorporate relevant multimedia, such as videos that can immerse the user right off. The trade-off, however, is that since your homepage serves as a landing page, which users navigate back to repeatedly, an intense or overly complex design could quickly become tiresome or overwhelming. Finding the right balance will be your key to creating a positive impact.

WHAT ARE THE TEXT COMPONENTS OF A COVER PAGE

Title and your name are two key components that should be incorporated into your cover design, no matter who your audience is. The title can be as simple as "portfolio" or "selected works." You can also go more creative and provide a name that defines your collection. In this case, make sure that the title accurately reflects the contents of your portfolio; otherwise, it will confuse your message. You may also want to consider including the range of years for your work. This can help the reader to understand the evolution of your skills and interests over time. Though, if you have been working for 20 years, including the range of years from 2004–2024 becomes irrelevant. If you are applying to graduate school, be sure to check the institution's requirements for the cover page. Some schools may require additional information, such as your university, degree, major or contact information.

Even on a portfolio website, your name remains a vital text component for the homepage, and though you probably won't have a title, you might include a professional brand. Also, a brief statement of your position can help visitors to quickly grasp the nature of your expertise, such as "Architect and Interior Designer," "Licensed Architect," or even something more general like "Architecture and Design." A significant difference between a standard cover page and a homepage is the presence of a navigation panel on a website. This essential tool must be designed with visibility, understandability, and intuition in mind. What exactly should be included in the navigation menu is discussed later in this Step.

DO consider a homepage statement that would encapsulate your design philosophy.

WHAT TO KEEP IN MIND WHEN DESIGNING A COVER PAGE

There are several principles you should follow when creating a cover page or homepage design. These are:

- **simple layout**
- **strong composition**
- **clear visual hierarchy**
- **cohesive design**

HOW TO ACHIEVE A SIMPLE COVER LAYOUT

There is often a tendency to over complicate the design of a cover page. Instead of crowded or over decorated designs that often convey an unprofessional or desperate impression, focus on a strong image or concept. One way to describe this strategy is to think of your cover page as a billboard — something that must be quickly and easily understood. This mindset should then guide you to use simplicity and clarity in your design. Simplicity doesn't imply lack of effort.

On the contrary, simple design is achieved through focus and intention. Lackluster or underdeveloped cover pages may appear simple but they can lack that clear intention.

HOW TO ACHIEVE
A STRONG COMPOSITION

DO think about highlighting specific aspects of your projects, such as showing close-up details.

A strong composition can also be a simple composition. Clean and minimalistic patterns create a clear focal point and deliver a sense of balance in the design. Following visual principles like the rule of thirds and symmetry will help you to achieve the overall harmony of your cover page. While it is never a mistake to apply a static-centered or symmetric composition to your cover page, it may lack an overall power and dynamism that may help set your portfolio apart from others. Creating an off-center composition with asymmetric balance can add a layer of uniqueness and sophistication to your design that, if done well, engages your audience from the start.

HOW TO ACHIEVE
A CLEAR HIERARCHY

DO consider including a blank spread right after the cover, and just before the back cover.

The primary focus should unquestionably be on your imagery. And whether you opt to create tension between your imagery and title or let your image take center stage and all your text components exist as a subordinate layer – that is on you to decide. In the first scenario, however, you ought to find appropriate balance and not over complicate your composition; otherwise, the viewer's eyes are going to dart around without a clear focal point. In the case of a dominant image, you need to be careful about not burying your text components too much, otherwise they may go easily unnoticed if not strategically placed or highlighted. Whatever your design choices, certain aspects remain appropriate to a cover: your title and name should be clearly legible with proper contrast and readable with an appropriately sized font.

COVER PAGE EXAMPLES

The cover employs simple, scattered images as a teaser for the content inside. The author's attention to composition and proportion indicates a sense of spatial relationships.

portfolio'23
anna gabitova

ANNA GABITOVA

The author uses an abstract image to pique curiosity. The centrally positioned object is carefully scaled in the mundane backdrop yet still conveys a notable impact.

ALI ISMAIL KARIMI

A full bleed image of a rich visualization effectively showcases the author's creativity and technical expertise, and highlights his attention to detail.

BURAK CELIK

The author's cover manifests a sense of depth and space through a delicately shaded soft drawing. The textual information mirrors the softness with discreet adjustments in sizing and coloring.

ELIZABETH ADEBAYO

The authors' design sensibilities are reflected through careful distribution of a contemporary, simple typeface, resulting in a clean and professional aesthetic.

DANIYAR MAGADIEV

ABDELAZIZ AWAD

The author's skill for visual representation is presented by the marvelous illustration. The full-bleed illustration's strong contrast immediately grabs attention while still maintaining focus on textual information.

COVER PAGE EXAMPLES

GABRIEL NUNES

The monochromatic color palette emanates a contemporary and refined ambiance through a captivating project image at a dynamic angle. The balance of other objects allows the viewer to easily digest information.

IMAGE BY LUCIA KRIVÁ

A evocative, monochromatic photograph on the cover suggests the author's unique lens through which she perceives architecture in the world.

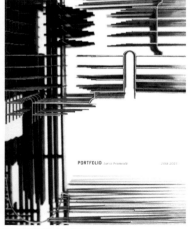

IMAGE BY LUCAS DENMEADE

The author applies model photography that highlights both his model-making and compositional skills, and emphasizes the model's unique features.

17-

A minimalistic cover thrives on an off-centered layout, strategically placing gestures representing the contents along the spine to captivate and engage the viewer's curiosity.

-22

ILIA ALADOV

This cover features a well-placed and high-contrast gestural representation of the contents, giving the viewer a sense of the author's compositional skill.

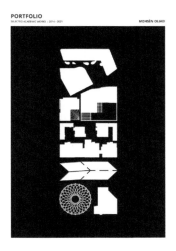

MOHSEN OLIAEI

The author effectively and provocatively uses superimposing techniques with content imagery, displaying visual skills and imagination and evoking curiosity.

JEK KEE LIM

WHY A COVER SHOULD
HAVE A COHESIVE THEME

The theme running through the body of your portfolio helps to tie all your content together. And your cover page shouldn't be left out of the established system. This means that the layout elements, such as typography, color palette and possibly even a grid system, should maintain consistency across both the portfolio content and the cover. Achieving this holistic approach will present you as an individual with a keen eye for detail as well as an understanding of the value of cohesive design.

RESUME —

HOW TO PRESENT
A RESUME

Whether a resume is a separate document from your portfolio or not, it is an essential part of your presentation. A resume is a short synopsis of your education, experience and other qualifications formatted on one page or, at the most, two. Don't feel obligated to include every single accomplishment. Leave those for a more extensive CV. Include only what is the most relevant and what fit the job description. Your resume should be concise, precise and, above all, truthful. Being honest with yourself when writing a resume is a fundamental approach that must not be compromised. Your credibility will vanish when the prospective employer finds out you stretched the truth.

DO be honest with yourself when writing your resume, as your credibility is at stake.

Portfolio websites offer more freedom for the resume location. Whether it's a separate page labeled "resume" in the navigation menu or integrated within the content on the "about me" page, always make sure it is easily accessible. If attached, make the resume downloadable in PDF format to allow your prospective employers or users to save or print the document if it's needed.

DON'T prioritize creativity over functionality when creating a resume.

DO make the key information bold to bring focus and ease navigation.

The key to organizing your resume lies in a clean and easily identifiable structure. The reader should be able to skim through the resume to get a broad view and then read for a more detailed understanding of information, such as work experience. An effective way to structure your information is to divide the page into two or three columns at the most. Establish a distinct hierarchy by using variations of font size and weights for section headings, job titles, and descriptions so the reader can quickly distinguish information. It's also important to keep the alignment consistent so it is predictable and easier to navigate. Left-aligned text is the best alignment to use as it ensures an uninterrupted flow of text and an effortless reading experience. Also, white space is another tool you shouldn't forget. Integrate it into your layout to help the reader focus on the content. Lastly, bear in mind that maintaining a visual consistency between your resume and portfolio design will keep your message intact.

DO make your resume style cohesive with your portfolio.

Simple graphics such as lines can help the reader distinguish each section and help the overall readability if used thoughtfully. But you must use them carefully and do not rely on their function since an overabundance of such graphics like bars, bullet points and symbols can make the layout cluttered and compete with your essential information. Instead, prioritize the use of white space to organize your content in a clear and concise manner.

WHAT ARE THE
RESUME COMPONENTS

A resume should include several sections, which can be adjusted for relevancy or tailored to an audience. Typically, these sections are:

- photograph – optional
- contact information
- short summary – optional
- education – academic history, extra-curriculum activities...
- experience – employment history, internships...
- accomplishments – awards, recognitions, exhibitions...
- skills – softwares, digital fabrication, physical modeling...
- hobbies, interests and languages

WHY OR WHY NOT TO INCLUDE YOUR PHOTO

If you plan to include a photograph on your resume, be sure that it conveys a sense of your personality and identity, captured in a serious and professional manner. However, be aware of the fact that a photograph is not a requirement for your resume and neither for your portfolio. The primary focus should be on showcasing your skills, potential and creative identity. Talent is not defined by factors such as race, gender or photogenic appeal, so let your work speak for itself. Allow a reviewer to see your work before they see you.

WHAT TO INCLUDE IN CONTACT INFORMATION

The first information on your resume is your contact information that should include your full name and your address. Depending on your cultural norms, you might also choose to include your pronouns or your nationality. Following that, provide your contact details, such as your phone number, email address /better a professional one, if you have one/, and web page URL, if you have a website. Additionally, you may include a LinkedIn profile that is up-to-date, to provide a more comprehensive overview of your professional journey.

DO add an email contact link to your "about me" web page.

*DON'T include an
Instagram profile
of your resume,
as Instagram is
a social platform
and not a
professional one.*

Incorporating a short summary at the beginning of your resume can be a great opportunity to connect with your audience in a narrative way. This paragraph is a brief statement spanning just a few lines and aims to outline who you are as a professional in a quick overview. To make a powerful impact, begin by articulating your professional identity, followed by highlighting a few relevant top skills — whether soft or hard — and any experience that may support your statement. Lastly, be sure to convey why you are an ideal candidate for the job opening. Note that while you should use the first person, you may consider leaving out personal pronouns such as "I" to maintain a brief professional tone.

Besides the short summary, you may have the opportunity to create a bio summary that allows you to introduce yourself in more detail. The bio summary is typically used on a portfolio website, but it's also acceptable within your standard portfolio. In that case, it's best to locate it on a separate page, adjacent to the resume, to provide an in-depth introduction. For a portfolio website, you can create a simple "about" page to introduce yourself. To allow your audience to grasp key aspects quickly, aim for brevity, and limit your bio summary to one or two paragraphs offering a snapshot of your personal and professional journey. Unlike the resume summary, the bio summary allows you to use a more personal and conversational tone to facilitate the connection between you and your audience. When writing a bio summary, use these basic questions as a guide:

Who are you? •
What are you doing? •
What is your expertise? •
How does your experience distinguish you? •
What would you like to do next? •

RESUME EXAMPLES

CLAUDIA CRESPO

Author uses various font attributes and text justifications to establish a distinct hierarchy. Additionally, the photo is carefully placed at a modest scale, ensuring a balanced and professional presentation.

MOHSEN OLIAEI

This resume layout separates each section into four columns to ensure clear organization. The author skillfully uses the grid to break free from its pattern, enhancing the overall appeal.

TEXT BY LUCAS DENMEADE

A unique strategy employing mirrored paragraphs at the spine, formatted with a clear, simple text hierarchy, offers a refreshing and effortlessly navigable reading experience.

PROFILE /

ELISSA SUDARGO

A concise, single-column resume layout, complemented by ample white space, evokes a modern and fresh aesthetic. The brief summary on the facing page contributes to a well-rounded presentation.

WHAT TO INCLUDE
IN EDUCATION

In the education section, start with your most recently attended schools and the years you attended, along with your earned degrees and certifications. If you are still a student or a recent graduate looking for an internship, you may also include the high school you attended to provide a fuller background. However, as you progress in your professional development, the value of high school details becomes negligible. In addition to educational institutions, you should provide more specific information on your major, minor and perhaps even GPA /only if you're a student or a recent graduate, and only if it's higher than 3.5/. To bring depth to your educational profile, list any extracurricular clubs, charitable groups or Greek organizations in which you participated or had a leadership role. If necessary, you may add brief descriptions of the educational institutions or programs and other organizations to provide clarity.

DO order your resume in reverse chronological order, beginning with your most recent event.

WHAT TO INCLUDE IN
WORK EXPERIENCE

The experience section is the core of your resume as it provides a detailed account of your professional background, which is why employers often prioritize this section over others. So to start this section, begin by listing all the firms and companies you've worked for, the most recent first, including the months and years of employment. Be sure to include the positions you held along with brief descriptions of your responsibilities and the roles you performed. If you don't have any or have limited professional work experience, you should include all possible paid and unpaid work experience, such as internships, roles in student organizations, or even summer jobs in small diners. This will demonstrate your ability to work and your sense of responsibility. To give a fuller impression of your experience, describe your roles as specifically as you can, using vivid,

DO avoid overly complicated explanations or jargon that may hinder reader comprehension.

active verbs such as "Created a design," "Collaborated with," or "Directed project." Lastly, keep in mind that the more professional experience and knowledge you gain, the more decisions you have to make about what to include and what to leave off in this section, which depends on what is relevant to each audience.

WHAT TO INCLUDE IN ACCOMPLISHMENTS AND AWARDS

This section offers a prime opportunity to distinguish yourself from other candidates. Include any relevant distinctions, exhibitions, recognition awards or any other citations you've received which can bolster your profile, such as best student work of the year. Also research publications, honor roll awards and scholarships can impress a potential employer or academic institution. Be sure to provide details about each award or accomplishment, such as its title, year and a brief description of its purpose, level of recognition or what achievement you were specifically awarded for.

WHAT TO INCLUDE IN SKILLS

DON'T rank your skills. Such self-ratings are subjective and unreliable.

The skills section is a place where you highlight both your technical and workplace skills, that is, your hard and soft skills. There are several ways to organize this section, but the most effective way is to group your skills by primary functions such as 3D modeling: Revit, Rhinoceros or Rendering: Vray, Lumion. You can also include additional skills such as language proficiency or any other area of expertise that demonstrates that you are a candidate who is well-rounded, talented or curious. While it's good to highlight your strengths, avoid exaggeration and always be truthful about your abilities. Even small deceptions are a red flag.

WHAT TO INCLUDE
IN HOBBIES AND INTERESTS

Categories like your hobbies and interests allow you to reveal more about your personality, how you spend your free time, and what you are passionate about. However, while these categories may help to establish a personal connection between you and your audience, they generally don't carry significant weight in a professional resume. You should only include this section if you have limited professional experience and skills or hobbies that are relevant to the job, such as photography or digital art. In such cases, adding a hobbies and interests section may help to strengthen your resume.

DO ask permission before you list people as references.

DESIGN STATEMENT —

HOW TO PRESENT
A DESIGN STATEMENT

A design or artist statement is becoming a popular portfolio component. It serves as a means to offer your prospective employers, admissions personnel or clients insight into who you are as a designer, what motivates you and what you value most in your work. For a professional portfolio, strive for a brief yet comprehensive paragraph, ideally spanning four to eight sentences. In an academic portfolio, you may be required to add a little bit more detail to showcase the depth of your design thinking. When writing it, keep in mind these questions:

DON'T use your statement to tell a college or a professional firm what you expect from them.

- **What do you want to say as a designer?**
- **Where is your inspiration coming from?**
- **Where is your work headed?**

A design statement is usually located at the beginning of the portfolio, as a way of introducing yourself. Typically, it

DO check the spelling on your resume.

is placed before the resume page, or along with the resume /but only if you don't have a short summary/. Approach the visual representation of your design statement much like you would a resume, prioritizing functionality over aesthetics. A text block formatted with a reasonable width and ample white space on a page is perhaps the most effective method. If you want to infuse a little more appeal, consider offsetting your text block from the center, for instance.

▬ TABLE OF CONTENTS

A table of contents serves as a helpful tool for your audience to quickly navigate and reference your projects. But, there is more to it than that. First off, it shouldn't be ignored and thought of it as a functional component to plug in at the end of your process. Secondly, it's an opportunity to inject a fresh idea to your overall design. You want your contents to cohere with the overall portfolio but that doesn't stop you from expanding your established design. A simple row design is functional and easy to use, but there are various design techniques to experiment with when creating your table of contents:

images as content previews •
icons representing the content •
different weights and sizes of font /bold, large/ •
different use of grid •
unique alignment •

Note, the decision to include a table of contents depends on the length of your portfolio and may not add much value if you are presenting only a few projects.

TABLE OF CONTENTS EXAMPLES

PROJECTS

Web Portfolio

CLAUDIA CRESPO

A distinct level of hierarchy and generous white space give the layout a sense of organization. Additionally, the author smartly uses a QR code to point to further work through a website access.

Introducing each project through an icon representing its essence can provide a fresh approach to content. Also, the obvious square grid adds a contemporary touch that complements the stylish icons.

CONTENT

IMAGES BY RYAN TUCKER

This design utilizes a simple,
bold typeface to create a striking
effect. The starkness of the page
guarantees that the design is
anything but boring.

LUCIA KRIVÁ

Adding a visual summary of
projects as a content preview
allows the viewer to get a glimpse
of what's to come. The horizontal
alignment turns the portfolio into
a story.

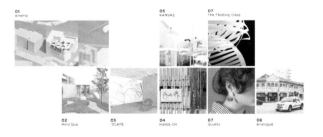

CONTENT /

ELISSA SUDARGO

For a portfolio website, the navigation menu on the home page serves as your table of contents. While a navigation menu is a condensed version of contents, its design holds central importance. There are no strict norms for navigation design, as it largely depends on the structure and design aims of your website. Whether you opt for a minimalistic horizontal menu at the top with a stylishly designed drop-down menu, a full-screen overlay menu that appears after a user clicks on a hamburger icon, a grid menu with interactive hover effects, or a split-up menu that divides the screen into sections — clarity, accessibility, visibility and ease of location should always be prioritized. If your website is designed with more complexity, or the menu alone doesn't provide enough clarity, you should always consider secondary navigation. This navigation can either encompass broader categories or simply repeat the primary navigation menu in an accessible way.

DO consider providing text with a visual gallery menu. It will help users to understand their choices.

INTRODUCTORY PROJECT PAGE —

HOW TO DESIGN AN INTRODUCTORY PROJECT PAGE

As you are stringing projects together, it becomes evident that you'll need to visually distinguish each project so that viewers can easily identify where each one begins. The introductory page serves a dual purpose: first, clearly separating your projects and second, providing a brief glimpse of the project's essence. Given that these pages mark a gateway into each project, design each with an eye-catching appeal that establishes a tone for what follows.

You can take a variety of approaches to mark the starts of your new projects in a compelling way. For instance, a minimal but generous tactic is using the full spread to feature an eye-catching image that best represents the project. Alternatively, you can captivate your audience with a more unconventional approach by using a section divider that introduces the project with a well-crafted paragraph, followed by traditional introductory pages. These could be a spread that, say, features a full-bleed image on the right page and a center-aligned block of text on the left, clean with a clear hierarchy. Regardless of how you design it, remember to apply principles of similarity and create a consistent presentation throughout your introductions while allowing for a distinct identity for each.

The introductory pages ought to be informative yet brief, emphasizing key aspects of the project. To provide the necessary context and essential details about your project, use the components below:

project title •
project number – optional •

Then, if the project is academic, continue with critical project details such as:

project site location •
year/semester – optional •
course name /especially if academic portfolio/ •
course instructor – optional •
additional credits /if a collaborative design/ •

Or, if you did your project as a professional, continue with critical project details such as:

project site location and size •
project completion date •
client/owner •
project cost – optional •
team members, project collaborators •

Also, every introduction should include:

> • **short project description**
> • **key words – optional**

Lastly, as with every page in the portfolio, include this on your introduction pages:

> • **navigation text /running header/ – optional**
> • **folio /page number/**

HOW TO APPROACH
A PROJECT TITLE

When coming up with a name for your project, your goal is to make it specific to the project itself while also being brief and captivating. Once you find a title, give it hierarchy and make it stand out with size and font weight, for example. You can also experiment with different alignments or spacing to set it apart from the rest of the information. Additionally, you can explore different layout options for positioning your title. The top-center area is typically the most effective for titles as it naturally draws the eye. However, if you want to add more visual interest, you could try placing your project name off-center using asymmetrical arrangements.

DO avoid using a broad, generic project title that can be applied to a wide range of projects.

WHEN TO USE
A PROJECT NUMBER

Adding project numbers to your portfolio is an optional yet valuable idea, especially if your portfolio is a longer one. The numbers indicate at a glance the quantity and scope of your portfolio and help with navigation. When designing, make sure to give the numbers an appropriate level of hierarchy, which commonly gets confused. The project numbers are, indeed, closely linked to the project title, but they should not be overly emphasized to the point of drawing attention away from the title or the content on the page. Instead, use the same or maybe even a lower level of hierarchy to maintain an orderly flow. Although typically a project number is placed in close proximity to the project title, don't shy away from less conventional approaches like positioning it at the bottom of a page or on the facing page.

HOW TO DISPLAY
PROJECT DETAILS

DO format the project details in a consistent manner across all projects in your portfolio.

The details of your projects, such as project location, completion date, course name, instructor, etc., are supposed to give a broader understanding of the project before delving into the specific project description. To clearly convey that these details are related and represent a unified set of information, you should group them together. Also, you want to give this group more emphasis than the project description. This hierarchy need not to be a dramatic, with bold or large type adjustments. Even a subtle treatment like different leading, italic font style, or paragraph alignment and positioning can help distinguish the details text from the description.

WHAT TO INCLUDE
IN PROJECT DETAILS

While most project details like site location and list of collaborators are straightforward, some have a few bends. For instance, the year of completion should always be listed for a project, but in the case of an academic portfolio, you might be required to also list the academic year when studio projects were completed /for instance, freshman or second-year studio/. However, in a professional portfolio, such information is less relevant. Employers view your projects as a demonstration of your skills and potential abilities for their company, and they are less concerned with the details of your academic development. The purpose of a professional portfolio is not to serve as a record of your college progression but rather to showcase your relevant work experience and potential.

Also, some academic institutions may have a policy that grants the instructor a claim in the ownership of the work, while others may have different policies in place. Therefore, it is vital to understand the ownership policies of your institution before you send out your portfolio and to list the project instructor in your project details if necessary.

HOW TO WRITE
A SHORT DESCRIPTION

A project description is an overview of the project with brief but informative details which highlight your ideas and their development. Depending on the complexity and scope of the project, it's best to aim for brevity and limit yourself to about 200 words or fewer to describe your project without overwhelming your reader with unnecessary details.

DO make clear your own responsibilities, when describing a team project.

Even though project descriptions seem to take center stage, these paragraphs are often only read when the reader becomes interested in the project and wants to know more. Therefore, the project description should offer somewhat more profound information about the project; in other words, it should bridge any gaps that the visuals may leave out. These gaps may include the ephemeral, experiential or procedural aspects of a presented design. Below are several practical ideas on how to write your project description:

• reduce text as much as possible; what remains has impact
• convey information that is not obvious from the image
• use direct language

If you feel uncertain about how to approach your project description, start with an explanation of the client's needs or the academic assignment brief. Consider adding any special challenges and limitations encountered in the project. Then, continue to your own concept, key design ideas, and process. The ending sentence should summarize your perspective on the project results and/or what you learned from it.

HOW TO APPROACH
KEYWORDS

DON'T use broad, general keywords that can overlook distinctive project features.

Keywords are short phrases that provide a quick insight into your work so that the viewer can quickly identify the project's key themes and concepts without having to read the project description. Including keywords is not obligatory, though their effectiveness makes them a valuable addition to your portfolio. The same idea holds true for your website portfolio where incorporating keywords is not an absolute necessity, but it has the additional advantage of making your portfolio easily searched and discovered.

The effectiveness of keywords resides in their brevity and their accuracy and specificity to your project. For instance, if you are presenting a K-12 school project with a diverse program, instead of using generic keywords like "school" or "educational institution," use more specific phrases consisting of 2–4 words that describe key concepts such as "Diversity of public spaces" or "Accessible tie-in to existing building." When creating your keywords, you can also highlight the unique aspects of your project, such as "Visibility from the street" or "Library as studio approach."

Similar to the project details, you should format keywords to quickly differentiate them as a distinct information group. The level of hierarchy for your keywords is flexible, but for a logical flow and efficiency, it's best to place your keywords on the same level as your project details. From there you can experiment further with different formats to achieve a visual clarity, such as the use of a bullet points or a different font style and weight.

HOW TO APPROACH
NAVIGATION TEXT

In a standard PDF portfolio, navigation text, also called a "running header," serves as a guide that informs your readers what part of your portfolio they are viewing. While there is no need to include navigation text in sample portfolios, you may consider it for a full portfolio to facilitate navigation. Typically, navigation text designates a portfolio category or a specific project or both. This text should be easy to locate at the top of each page with possible exceptions such as a full-bleed. However, you can also deviate from these conventions and place it vertically at the edge of side margins, for instance.

DO consider using all caps text for navigation text and/or captions.

In the realm of portfolio websites, the navigation text simply represents the navigation menu and includes the links that take users to different parts of your website. The language used in this text should clearly indicate the user's current location and should present the primarily portfolio categories, such as "About," "Resume," and "Projects," etc. Depending on how you categorize your content, you may also have subcategories placed in drop-down menus. However, be careful not to create too many links as it can overwhelm and confuse users. Remember that users usually expect to reach their desired destination within two or three clicks.

DO ensure clarity and accessibility in your navigation menu. When an item is chosen or hovered over, it should be highlighted.

HOW TO DESIGN
A FOLIO

Page numbers, also known as folios, are pivotal in organizing your portfolio as they allow your readers to quickly locate specific content. While there is room for creativity in their formatting, make sure folios are placed in a visually accessible location and are easily identified yet not overly distracting. The most practical choice, therefore, is to place them in the upper or lower corners on the outer edge of your margins. However, considering folios are not the most essential information, you can opt for more unique locations, such as along the outside margins or at the center of the top or bottom margins. In cases of full bleed pages, you may omit the folio as an occasional absence won't disorient your viewer.

— PROJECT PAGE

HOW TO DESIGN
PROJECT PAGES

DON'T overwhelm your audience with excessive details. Instead create a focused narrative.

As you have guided your audience through the gateway of your project, it's time to immerse them in more comprehensive views. This includes supporting diagrams, sketches, plans, sections, elevations, renders and photographs of models. There is no absolute measure for the ideal number of project pages, as it depends on the format of your portfolio and the complexity of your project. Nevertheless, it's worth maintaining brevity to keep the viewer engaged. Confining your project pages to a spread or two should be sufficient to provide ample information and convey your project's depth. Although your curation should be finalized, you may be tempted to add more to show your full investment in the project, making your project pages tedious and the viewing experience passive. Present only the imagery that best conveys the idea behind the project and provides fresh information. For complex projects, focus on key drawings. For instance, if you present an apartment building with multiple stories, include only the floor plan or plans representing your best ideas. Or, if the section drawings are more informative than the elevations, prioritize those.

HOW TO PACE
A PROJECT STORY

To pace out your content, think of it as a story that you want to share with your audience. A commonly used approach is to begin strongly with an impressive visualization, gradually introduce supporting visuals to provide depth and context and conclude with another impactful image. However, a chronological approach might be equally powerful if you have quality conceptual sketches that can impress the viewer right from the start. Another option is a combined approach, where renderings are accompanied by associated sketches, floor plans, or sections. In this case, ensure that you link the relevant imagery together so that the audience understands the project accurately. Use the visual principles in previous Steps to create an effective and engaging layout.

Beyond your main imagery, consider other visuals:

- **technical drawings**
- **model photography**

The elements listed below can help clarify your ideas to the audience:

- **captions**
- **callouts and leading lines**
- **other graphics**

HOW TO PRESENT
TECHNICAL DRAWINGS

Technical drawings are a vital presentation of your technical proficiency and structural understanding, which is highly valued throughout architecture and particularly in construction. Technical drawings such as construction details may not boast the same visual appeal as other images in your portfolio, but if they are well made and present a unique structural solution, they will set you apart from other candidates. However, if you are not technically proficient in that area, it's better to not include them. Presenting default technical drawings just to fulfill a presumed requirement will not impress anyone and could cast a shadow upon your more skilled work. Best to be honest with yourself!

DO give your technical drawings appropriate scale to show every detail.

DO consider a separate section of full CAD drawings, especially if you are in construction fields.

When presenting technical drawings, pay extra attention to the line weights, hatches, and other details included in the drawing to ensure that the information is clearly conveyed. Also, because the scale can significantly impact the resolution and readability of your drawings, you need to make sure that your drawings retain their good quality. Lastly, remember that saving your line drawings as PDF or PNG files will help preserve the quality of the line edge in your drawing.

HOW TO PRESENT MODEL PHOTOGRAPHY

While much has been covered in Step 2 about photographing models, there are additional techniques you might use to enhance your presentation. Beyond proper lighting, a clean background and varied angles, you should also focus on image composition. To achieve the best results, you should use framing techniques, particularly the rule of thirds, to direct the viewer's attention to specific parts of the model. You can apply this rule during post-processing by cropping the image to align key moments along the grid lines and intersections. Let yourself further experiment with sharp focus, background blur, filters, or other effects to add a layer of specific mood or atmosphere. However, use these techniques sparingly to maintain a professional and consistent look across all images of the project to ensure a cohesive visual narrative.

HOW TO USE CAPTIONS

Captions are concise, specific image descriptions that should be handled much like your project descriptions — describe not the obvious but rather what can't be realized from the imagery itself. For example, instead of using "Sections" or "Kitchen Interior," expand and clarify the content to provide a better understanding of the image, such as "NorthWest Sections" or "Kitchen Interior view from the adjacent living room."

MODEL PHOTOGRAPHY EXAMPLES

NICHOLAS MACINTYRE

With close-up shots you can emphasize intricate details, textures, and materiality of your model, allowing viewers to appreciate the craftsmanship and subtleties that might be overlooked in broader perspectives.

CSENGE KIRÁLY

Outdoor model photography can take advantage of different lighting and angles to articulate unique qualities of the model.

JEK KEE LIM

Including people, furniture, or other recognizable objects in your physical model helps to convey the scale and proportion of the model.

CHARLOTTE BASCOMBE

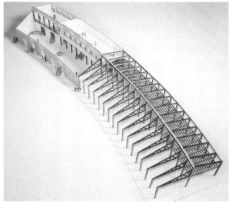

CHARLOTTE BASCOMBE

Offering diverse perspectives, including overhead and eye-level views, fosters a comprehensive grasp of the design's essence — capturing both the overarching concept of your project and its human experiential dimension.

Exploring various light placements and intensities opens up possibilities for creating impactful shadows, infusing your model with depth and dimension to effectively highlight architectural form.

ALI ISMAIL KARIMI

One important aspect when formatting captions is to design them in a way that doesn't compete with the image itself. This is easily achieved with the use of a subtle font that is easy to read. Commonly, captions exist right next to the corresponding image, but they can also be grouped together and placed in the corner, for instance. In this case, you need to clearly indicate each caption's image location, such as "top left" or "below." However, grouping captions together on website portfolios can introduce challenges, as various factors may easily misalign the arrangement of images and confuse the intent of the captions. Therefore, it's best to focus on the function first and place captions next to the images to provide a seamless viewing experience.

DO bear in mind that captions are more likely to be read by your audience than your project description.

HOW TO USE CALLOUTS AND LEADING LINES

Callouts are another type of textual image description whose purpose may resemble captions. However, unlike captions, which provide broader context, callouts draw attention to specific features of an image and highlight their importance. Callouts are accompanied by leading lines that link them to the exact area of the image they refer to. Make sure to place callouts next to the relevant image to support a visual connection. If you are dealing with a larger image, such as a full bleed, be sure to establish visual prominence and readability through adequate type contrast in a way that doesn't interfere with the primacy of the imagery. Alternatively, you can also use a simple box in which you insert your callout text.

DON'T use circles and bubbles for the callout. Stay professional.

Leading lines can be represented in full or dotted form and may end with an arrow or bullet point to further emphasize the particular spot in the image. Don't forget to set up appropriate line weights so your leading lines neither overpower nor blend in with the image.

DON'T use callouts excessively. It can distract from your imagery.

*DON'T include
software used
in the project.
It's unnecessary.
Technical skills
are revealed in the
imagery and listed
in your resume.*

Graphic scales are inherent to architectural drawings, but they don't necessarily have to accompany drawings in your portfolio. Since portfolios are not documents intended for construction purposes, it's generally understood that drawings may not always be to scale or require a scale. However, a drawing convention like a north arrow can be helpful, indeed, as it provides an orientation. If you do end up using any of these graphics, make sure they are in the appropriate proximity and maintained at a small but legible scale, so they serve their supportive role.

Whether to include software icons in your layouts or not is your decision. While it can offer a quick way for viewers to identify the software tools used in the project, it's worth considering that your resume already highlights your software proficiency. In addition, software icons could potentially clutter your layout. Moreover, recruiters in the field likely have a good understanding of the software tools used for a project, making this information redundant.

— EXTRAS

*DO include other
creative work. It
brings out your
distinctiveness
and adds a depth
to the audience's
perception.*

While your architectural design should be the primary focus of your portfolio, don't shy away from highlighting work beyond the architectural field. This section holds double significance when applying to academia as it offers a more holistic view of your creativity and skills. Remember that quality matters more than quantity. Select a few of the most outstanding photographs, sculptures, paintings, or any other work that aligns with your design thinking. Approach this section with the same thoughtful attention that you bring to the design of other project pages.

HOW TO PRESENT
RESEARCH

A theoretical project, such as a thesis or other research endeavor, carries significant weight in an academic portfolio. These projects reveal the intellect you've brought to a project, which reinforces your potential in architectural discourse. Given their often lengthy and dense nature, presenting these projects in an appealing visual manner can be daunting. To overcome this challenge, leverage all your visual aids, such as diagrams, charts or other analyses, to help the audience understand essential information or findings and conclusions. Additionally, if possible, try to condense it into an abstract summary. Lastly, reformat your text to align with the established aesthetics of your portfolio to make it appear seamlessly integrated — all part of your singular effort.

DO consider presenting your research. Use an excerpt or abstract of an extensive work.

THANK YOU AND CONTACT INFORMATION —

HOW TO END
A PORTFOLIO

As you reach the end of your portfolio, remember to bring your story or journey to a meaningful close. Expressing gratitude by including a "Thank you" note on the last page of your portfolio can go a long way in showing your appreciation for the time and attention of your audience. Another key element to include at the end of your portfolio is a "call to action." Encourage your audience to take further steps, such as contacting you through your email address, phone number and a link to your website where they can find a fuller display of work.

A portfolio website, however, doesn't provide you with the same opportunity to include a definitive last page or express the final word. But there are still effective ways to conclude your portfolio website. First, encourage your users to get in touch with you through the "Contact" page, which should be the last option in your navigation menu. Beyond this, you should consider including a link to the "Contact" page in the footer to allow your audience to access your contact information from anywhere on your website. Similarly, your "About me" page can also provide a clear call to action. Remember that for a nonlinear website, redundancy may be necessary to guide users effectively.

— COMMON MISTAKES

TOO MUCH SELF-PROMOTION
ON COVER PAGE

The order in which the objects are placed on your cover page can greatly affect the message you are trying to convey to your audience. In a portfolio design, making your name the most prominent element on the cover page may appear unprofessional or overly self-promoting /see common mistakes 1/. Such a hierarchical order is more appropriate for a well-known public figure. And so, presenting your name as a subordinate element and prioritizing the use of imagery might present you as a designer who lets your work speak for itself.

OVER-DESIGNED
OR NOT DESIGNED COVER

Architecture is a competitive, creative field, and your portfolio cover should reflect your design flair. An unimaginative, dull, or generic cover won't elevate your portfolio above others /see common mistakes 2/. In fact, it might turn your audience away before they even begin exploring your work.

On the other hand, while creativity is encouraged, your cover design should not take away from your overall professional presentation — it should captivate rather than distract. An excessively adorned cover with numerous images lacking purpose may risk losing the audience's interest right from the beginning /see common mistakes 3/. Remember that your portfolio cover is the first impression you'll make, so strive for a balance between creativity and professionalism.

DO experiment with the cover page composition to get to the right reflection of your design sensibility.

BORROWED IDEAS
ON THE COVER

There is nothing wrong with seeking design inspiration online. However, directly borrowing ideas from another successful cover page may have a counterproductive effect. A copied cover is more likely to be broadly applicable and may not accurately reflect your own unique style and approach. If you adopt someone else's idea, the designs within your portfolio may not match up with the expectations set by the cover page. Remember that your cover page is essentially a visual representation of your portfolio, and it should introduce your individuality and creativity. If you do end up using a template, you should customize it by experimenting with color, fonts, or even composition so you bring your unique sense of style to it.

POOR SELECTION OF
COVER IMAGE

Incorporating an image on the portfolio cover can be a powerful strategy to offer a preview of your design style and aesthetics right from the beginning. Nevertheless, if the chosen image is ineffective or unrelated to your work /see common mistakes 4,5/, it can derail your best intentions from the very beginning. Therefore, aim to select an image that has both an immediate impact and best represents the message you wish to convey about your architectural work.

DO think about altering an image, perhaps by cropping, to make your cover more impactful.

The impact of a resume is heavily reliant on its layout and formatting. Resumes should prioritize functionality over creativity. Without proper formatting /grid scheme, hierarchy, and negative space/, the text may appear cluttered and difficult to read and navigate /see common mistakes 6/. Also, the most relevant information may not stand out, which makes it challenging for recruiters to quickly grasp key details. If you focus on good readability, clear organization and formatting and emphasize the key points, your audience will be able to efficiently extract essential information.

DO avoid using both an icon and a word if they represent the same meaning. Use the one that works better.

Although creativity in your overall portfolio design is encouraged, in a resume, particularly, your design intentions should be more purposeful and functional. Therefore, you should refrain from overusing graphics that don't serve any purpose such as frames, boxes or other decorative graphics /see common mistakes 8/. In fact, they only distract the viewer from the actual information and can diminish the effectiveness of your resume more than one might anticipate.

While icons and symbols are commonly used to enhance visual appeal, you ought to be extra cautious about their effect. Overusing or repeating icons without a clear design purpose can easily lead to clutter and may give off an unprofessional or gimmicky impression /see common mistakes 7/. Rather, play it safe, prioritize clarity and simplicity over redundancy, and consider using simple words to convey information effectively instead of relying too heavily on icons.

RATING SKILLS
IN RESUME

> One easily avoidable error in a resume is the use of self-assessment rating for skills /see common mistakes 9/. This rating is often subjective and generally unreliable, as it's challenging to judge oneself fairly. Instead, provide only a simple, straightforward list of your skills without any form of assessment such as "RhinoCeros, Revit, Adobe Photoshop,..." and demonstrate your capabilities through the work presented in your portfolio. Allow your prospective employers or admission officers to evaluate your skills by themselves.

EXCESSIVE USE
OF TEXT

> A well-written explanation of your design process is undoubtedly beneficial, but it loses its value when the text becomes too long /see common mistakes 10/. Your audience, with their limited time and attention, is less likely to engage when confronted with overwhelming amounts of written content. Take this as an opportunity to show your writing discipline and creative focus by composing a concise description. Encourage your audience to seek more details about your project if they want to hear more.

REDUNDANCY OF
TEXT AND IMAGES

> When writing a text, particularly a project description or captions, you need to be attentive and not restate what is already apparent from the visuals /see common mistakes 11/. Such text won't add value and only becomes unnecessary filler content. For instance, labeling your project description paragraph with "a description" or using a caption that says

Do keep in mind that architecture is a visual discipline. Your primary focus should be on the visual representation.

"floor plan" or "photograph of model" is superfluous. Rather, provide additional context, explanations, and interpretations to deepen the viewer's understanding, such as "third story floor plan" or "projected shadows in late evening."

Likewise, including images that convey the same or similar information is a visual filler that doesn't contribute anything new to the audience's comprehension. To overcome this, choose an image that expands the representation of your idea rather than one that blurs your message with nearly duplicate content.

USE OF UNNECESSARY GRAPHICS

DO remove all unnecessary graphics. What remains is your message.

Creating a portfolio with a strong visual impact is an opportunity, but also it creates a responsibility for you to maintain a seriousness while being inventive and expressive. You should aim to captivate your audience with visually engaging layouts, but don't get carried away with unique graphics and visual effects such as obtrusive lines, drop shadows or gradients /see common mistakes 12,13/. The overuse or misuse of these graphics doesn't make your work more noticeable; instead, it might distract from it. So, keep away from their use and maintain restraint with a striking yet simple approach. Leverage visual design principles to emphasize your work and select a consistent aesthetic that mirrors your design values. Always remember that the visual layout of your portfolio should complement your work, not overpower it.

USE OF LINE BORDERS
AROUND DESIGN OBJECTS

There is no absolute rule against using line borders, but before you use them, consider visual principles along with the design goals of your portfolio. In situations where you need to separate two objects to prevent them from visually bleeding into each other, applying a border or fill box might help to create a visual separation. However, in many cases, it can be counterproductive as it creates a visual noise that distracts from the actual content /see common mistakes 14,15/. Consider using white space instead to create an invisible separation between the visual objects. This gives attention to the objects themselves.

DO remove borders and dividers. Instead, use white space to achieve separation.

POOR WEBSITE
NAVIGATION

Of all portfolio types, the website portfolio depends upon functionality the most. Poor website navigation can diminish the value of your work, as users struggle to navigate. This frustration may limit interest and turn users away. A typical problem is when your navigation menu provides too many options or categories /see common mistakes 16/. Having fewer categories that accurately represent the content of pages will streamline viewing experience.

Users also can lose interest or become irritated with nonstandard placements or less intuitive designs of navigation menus. For instance, concealed navigation menus or full-screen overlays are not immediately identifiable /see common mistakes 17/. Since such navigation menus require initial action to reveal their contents, users may become frustrated as they cannot easily access the navigation options. Therefore, if using non-conventional navigation menus, make sure they are easily accessed with a clear visual cue. Alternatively, you should consider adding a secondary navigational panel with a standard design.

COMMON MISTAKES

self-promotion

JEFF KAYDEN

selected works
2019/2023

PORTFOLIO
Jeff Kayden
2019/2023

1/

1/

1/ Overly self-promotional hierarchy for a cover page might give a limited or negative message.

When creating a cover page, you should balance between self-promotion and expression of your design identity.

SELECTED WORKS
2019/2023

jeff kayden

IMAGES THIS PAGE BY TREVOR RODGERS

not designed or over-designed

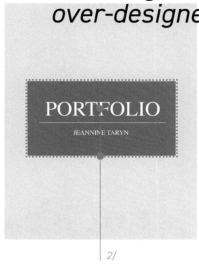

2/

3/

2/ *An uninspiring design with unimaginative composition, generic fonts, and unappealing colors won't stand out or reflect creativity.*

3/ *An excessively busy cover page with disjointed objects and stylish typeface may give off an unprofessional, amateurish impression.*

Invest your time to create a clean, simple but sophisticated composition. Showcase your design sensibilities with your image and typeface selection and your sense for dynamic arrangement.

COMMON MISTAKES

cover image

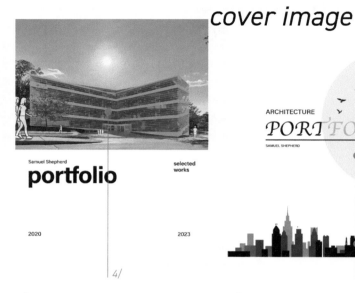

4/

5/

4/ An image that lacks power and fails to reveal interesting potential may not be able to capture the audience's attention effectively.

5/ A cover that lacks authenticity, original style or architectural perception will fail to stand out in a crowded field.

Make sure your cover image reflects qualities that align with your distinctive style and perception. Keep in mind that the placement and cropping of the image can also have a significant impact on your cover.

IMAGE BY TREVOR RODGERS

graphic overuse

6/ *Lack of formatting and hierarchy makes key information hard to find.*

7/ *Redundancy of information may lead to an unprofessional and cluttered look.*

8/ *Overuse of graphics can distract the reader from the content.*

9/ *Skill ratings are subjective and their meanings can differ from person to person.*

To create a professional resume, you should always create several columns to organize the information. Employ hierarchy, white space, and consistency to achieve a clean, easy-to-scan document.

COMMON MISTAKES

text overuse

04
scottish ambassador residence
Course Arhictecture Foundation
Location Washington DC
Year 2020

10/

11/

10/ *Verbose descriptions can feel overwhelming and discouraging for an audience to read through.*

11/ *Redundant or non-essential information takes up valuable space and detracts from the visual imagery.*

04
scottish ambassador residence
Course Arhictecture Foundation
Location Washington DC
Year 2020

Use concise project descriptions that highlight key aspects of your design process, concept and outcomes. Prioritize quality over quantity and avoid repeating information to save space and to highlight your visual presentation.

unnecessary graphics

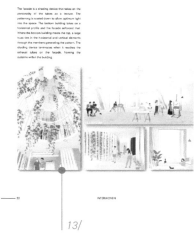

12/

13/

12/ Unnecessary use of graphics such as rectangles and decorative lines serve only as empty gestures and distract from the actual work.

13/ Including effects such as drop shadows may give the portfolio an amateurish or cluttered appearance.

To achieve a polished and professional look, you should eliminate all graphics that don't serve a purpose other than decoration. Instead, keep the layout simple and focused on your work.

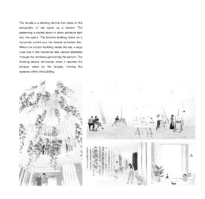

IMAGES THIS PAGE BY EMILY USSIA

COMMON MISTAKES

borders

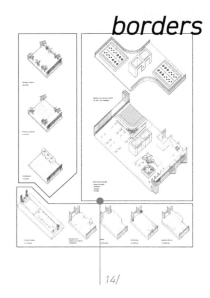

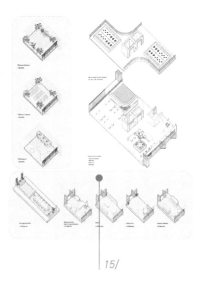

14/

15/

14/ *Excessive use of line borders can create visual clutter, ultimately distracting from the main content.*

15/ *Using fill boxes may lead to visual heaviness and unintentionally overemphasize some content.*

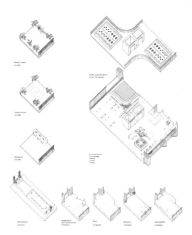

In many cases, removing borders and using white space contributes to a cleaner layout design. In some instances, you may have to downsize your visual objects to allow for enough negative space to create visual separation.

poor navigation

16/

17/

16/ Navigational menus with too many items can slow the user's exploration of the website.

17/ A hidden navigation menu can frustrate users by being hard to find. It can hinder access to critical content.

Be sure to prioritize a visible and easily accessible navigation menu. A simple structure with fewer items will streamline your user's experience.

IMAGES THIS PAGE BY LUCIA KRIVÁ

STEP 9

— CASE STUDIES

The previous Step drew together all the techniques, principles and tools and considered each of the components of the portfolio. Now this Step will look at real portfolio examples highlighting specific project pages and their introductions. These studies should help you search out and critically consider other examples as well. The real value of these case studies lies in helping you identify and understand the principles that make the portfolios effective, principles to use in your own expressive efforts.

WHAT TO
LOOK FOR

The following pages showcase excerpts from a diverse array of creative and successful portfolios. Each layout exemplifies the various elements, methods, and tools discussed in this Guide. The accompanying commentary begins to explore how these ideas have been integrated and what strategies were employed by each author listed below. Some of what follows is simple, some complex. Each represents a holistic achievement composed of many parts.

case study 1 - Maria Rybak •
case study 2 - Roberto Vargas •
case study 3 - Csenge Király •
case study 4 - Sai Raghav H •
case study 5 - Denis Zimakov •
case study 6 - Yoonseok Lee •
case study 7 - Paige Davidson •
case study 8 - Ali Ismail Karimi •
case study 9 - Elissa Sudargo •
case study 10 - Lucia Krivá •
case study 11 - Band Architecture •
case study 12 - Hamish Angus McAndrew •

PORTFOLIO EXAMPLES

portfolio by
Maria Rybak

*The author's approach showcases
a strong understanding of the
significance of visual elements
in communication, reflected in
the simple yet effective layout
compositions. The design strategies
presented in this portfolio exhibit
a remarkable balance, clarity, and
consistency throughout without
ever descending into monotony.*

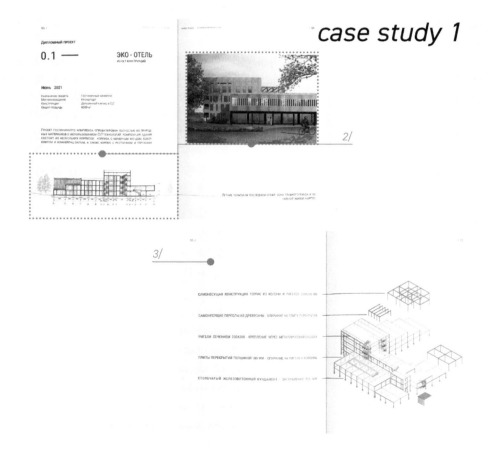

case study 1

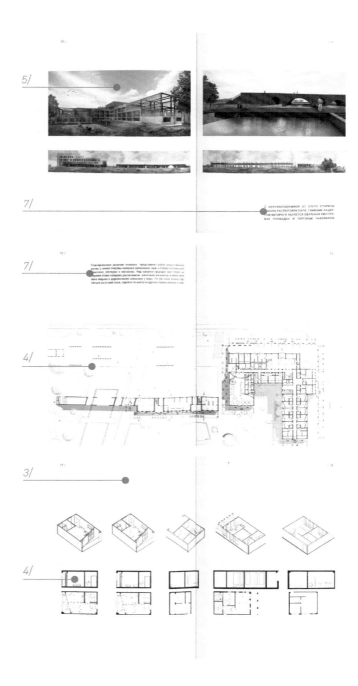

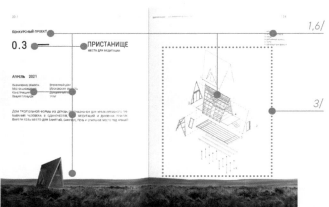

case study 1

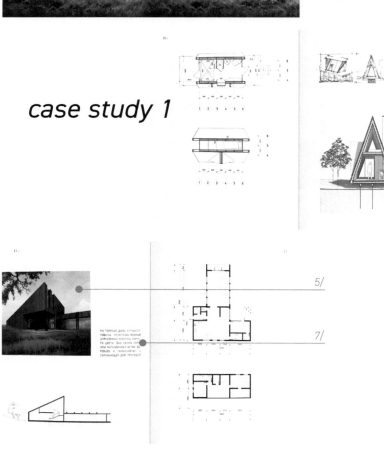

INTRODUCTORY PROJECT PAGES

The introduction pages are tacitly designed to maximize the use of available space on each spread. Despite the scattered layout, the author distributes the content objects with careful consideration of spacing, scale, and proportion, resulting in an engaging experience /1/. The powerful visualizations featured in the introductory pages are carefully balanced with intricate line drawings, creating a synergy where objects do not compete for importance but rather complement each other seamlessly /2/. The generous white space surrounding each visual object provides them a jewel-like quality, effectively making them stand out with prominence /3/. This technique is consistently present throughout, contributing to a cohesive and visually appealing presentation.

TEXTUAL ELEMENTS

The minimalistic typeface resonates with a modest layout, allowing the visual content to stand out. The author has strategically isolated the text into zones, creating a well-organized layout with a distributed focus across the spread /6/. The description block of text on project pages is always thoughtfully placed and proportioned to balance the visual attention in the layout /7/.

PROJECT PAGES

The project pages take a more lenient approach towards the grid structure. The author prioritizes the content objects over the grid system, conforming to the content's needs and then intuitively customizing alignments to different sizes and proportions to effectively convey information /4/. This technique works particularly successfully when presenting only one or two sets of drawings at a time, as it allows the audience to appreciate all the details in the rich visuals. The occasional interruption of simple but varied layouts with dramatic imagery contributes to a strong visual rhythm throughout the portfolio /5/. Despite the diversity in layouts, the author maintains visual consistency through a distinct representation style that unifies the portfolio down to the smallest details of line weights.

PORTFOLIO EXAMPLES

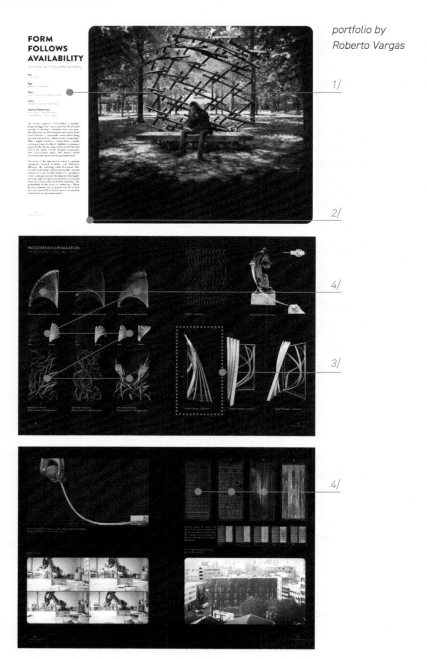

portfolio by
Roberto Vargas

*This portfolio layout employs
a systematic use of dynamic
alternation of grid and black-
and-white themes that keep the
audience engaged. This intentional
design choice not only contributes
to the author's stylish aesthetic but
also creates a sophisticated layout
that, yet, is easy to navigate.*

case study 2

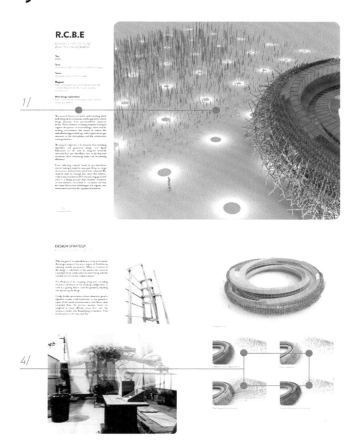

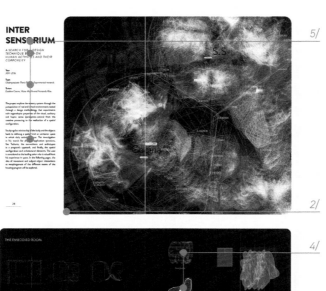

INTER
SENS RIUM

A SEARCH FOR A DESIGN
TECHNIQUE BASED ON
HUMAN ACTIVITIES AND THEIR
CORPOREITY

Year
2011–2016

Type
Undergraduate Thesis Design Experimental research

Tutors
Esteban Cásins, Víctor Muñoz and Fernando Ríos

The project explores the sensory system through the juxtaposition of real and virtual environments tested through a design methodology that experiments with organoleptic properties of the visual, auditory and haptic areas (perception extract from the creative processing to the realization of a spatial configuration.

Studying the relationship of the body and the objects leads to defining a spatial limit or container space in which daily activities occur. The investigation is his search for the application questions, like Taduma, the conventions and techniques in a pragmatic approach, and finally, the spatial configuration and architectural elements. The user is considered as the leading actor who is valued from his experience in space. In the following pages, the idea of movement and subject-object interactions or morphogenesis of the different means of the housing program will be explored.

5/

2/

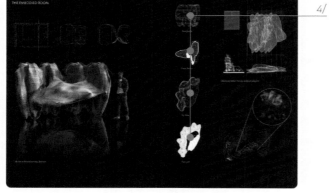

THE EMBODIED ROOM

4/

6/ KINÉSIC HOUSING MODULE

case study 2

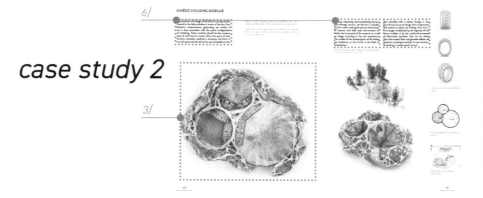

3/

INTRODUCTORY PROJECT PAGES

The strategic use of eye-catching imagery that extends across the spine and dominates the spread, while allocating careful proportion to project information, serves as a compelling invitation /1/. The structured and consistent approach to the introduction pages becomes a crucial navigational element, particularly as the following pages present diverse information. The author softens the imagery with a sleek technique of rounded corners, adding a pleasant graphical touch /2/.

TEXTUAL ELEMENTS

A bold project title set with a contemporary typeface is proportionally applied to balance the color-heavy imagery on the project introduction pages. The variety of font weights and strategic spacing between different text levels promotes a clear text hierarchy, effectively guiding readers through distinct levels of information /5/. The widths of the text block produce clear lines, which give a definition to a hidden grid in a subtle yet effective way /6/.

PROJECT PAGES

The sophisticated modular grid dynamically adapts from one project page to another and accommodates a diverse curation of images, creating an engaging narrative for each project. The grid's definition, however, is almost invisible, as the imagery has been cut out from its original background, losing its defined edge character /3/. This technique integrates the images seamlessly into the layout while also making them stand out. The placement and scale of individual images are thoughtfully considered to create threads of rows and columns, giving the layout a film sequence-like effect /4/. The alternating background color of the project pages adds a dramatic touch that complements the images, further enhancing their prominence and making them stand out with heightened visual impact.

PORTFOLIO EXAMPLES

portfolio by
Csenge Király

The contemporary design technique employed in this portfolio is fearlessly built on a hierarchical grid, asymmetry and bold typography. The background pallet correlating with earthy tones present in the imagery ties the presentation together. Overall, the author's distinctive approach creates a harmonious and refreshing presentation.

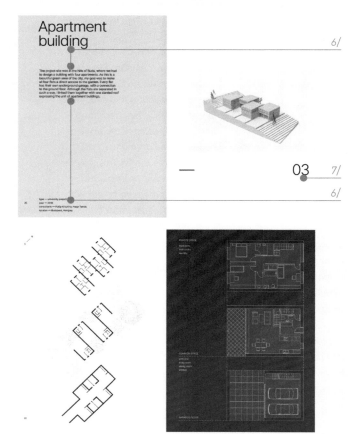

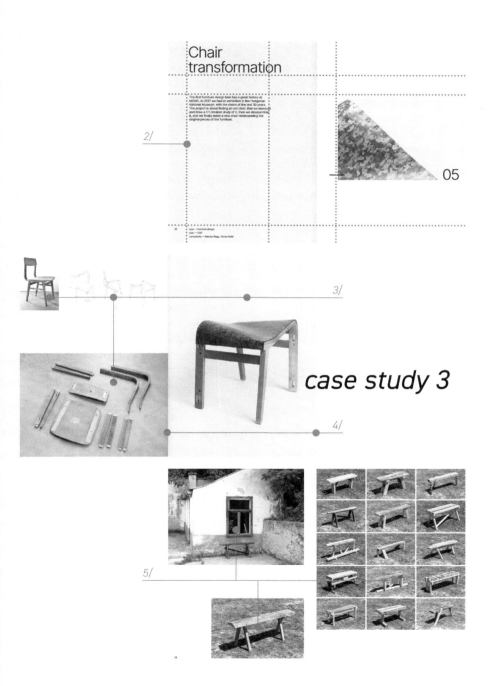

Chair
transformation

The first furniture design task has a great history at
MOME, in 2017 we had an exhibition in the Hungarian
National Museum, with the chairs of the last 30 years.
The project is about finding an old chair, that we measure
and draw a 1:1 detailed study of it, then we disassemble
it, and we finally make a new chair reinterpreting the
original pieces of the furniture.

2/

05

3/

case study 3

4/

5/

INTRODUCTORY PROJECT PAGES

The author establishes each new project category with a minimalistic colored section divider /1/. This color tone is then carried over to the introduction pages to continue a seamless transition between sections. Here, the author surprises with a fearless attitude of challenging conventional portfolio layouts. The substantial amount of negative space creates a peaceful and inviting environment, allowing the limited content, whether visual or textual, to stand out with clarity. To reinforce the clarity, the author maintains a consistent grid, along with the color coding /2/.

TEXTUAL ELEMENTS

The minimalist, soft layout is echoed in the light and unpretentious typography. The author makes use of a single typeface with varying font sizes to control hierarchical order. The strategic spacing and placement of textual elements contribute to an elegant and orderly design that guides the reader's attention /6/. The prominent yet unapparent project number location varies from project to project, contributing to a dynamic yet calm atmosphere /7/.

PROJECT PAGES

Despite the more relaxed and open grid structure in project pages, these layouts comprise a range of imagery and drawings with deliberate attention to proportion and proximity, resulting in a well-balanced hierarchical act that takes a viewer from one corner to another /3/. The effectively utilized grid violations, such as partial bleeds and elimination of spacing between imagery, inject a sense of energy and fluidity /4/. The sense of pace within the project pages presents a delicate balance between structure and creativity, resulting in a visually stimulating narrative flow. To add to the rhythmic atmosphere, the author also contrasts the free grid layout with a rigid alignment /5/. Such a departure from the conventional layout adds a touch of unpredictability and excitement to the overall design experience.

4/

case study 3

Workshops —

15
14
13
12
11

1/

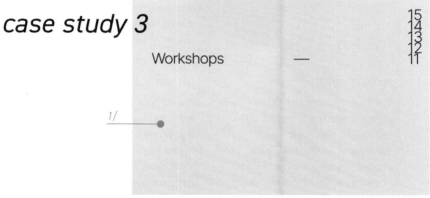

Chapel in the woods

— 11   3/

The idea of building a chapel was inspired by a university course about contemporary sacred art. The idea soon became a real project that took place in the city of Pannonhalma, in the forest of fok. Our chapel was non-denominational with no walls and roof. A mosaic altar is in the middle inspired by the dome of Galla Placidia.

type — building camp
year — 2016
project leaders — Áron Vass-Eysen, Tamás Bene, Zoltán Kórössváigyi
location — Pannonhalma, Hungary

PORTFOLIO EXAMPLES

portfolio by
Sai Raghav H

The author's use of a clean and straightforward design layout in a square format effortlessly balances a variety of imagery while ensuring easy absorption of information without overwhelming the viewers. Such a design strategy guarantees a visually appealing and informative portfolio that engages the audience from start to finish.

INTRODUCTORY PROJECT PAGES

The author starts the project with a confident approach of utilizing a high-quality, realistic, full-bleed image that instantly grabs the audience's attention and immerses them in the project /1/. The carefully selected imagery effectively depicts the project's essence in the best possible light, thereby establishing an engaging tone right away.

PROJECT PAGES

The following pages perfectly portray the author's careful negotiation with the format restrictions and the number of images. The project page always presents relevant pairs of drawings in an appropriate scale, enabling the viewer to appreciate the intricate details that the author has put into the artwork /2/. The author regulates the pace of the portfolio through a layout alternation. A full-bleed or crossover image that spans the entire spread creates a pause, but the visual rhythm picks up when a spread is divided into two pages using the edge of an image or a subtle background color change /3/.

TEXTUAL ELEMENTS

The author's attention to legibility is evident in a deliberate selection and application of typography. With a clear and expressive text hierarchy, the author uses a delicate font that maintains full legibility even against a vivid background /4/. The author's thoughtful approach also comes through in the callouts and legends, which have been adjusted to unify with the established font in the portfolio /5/.

case study 4

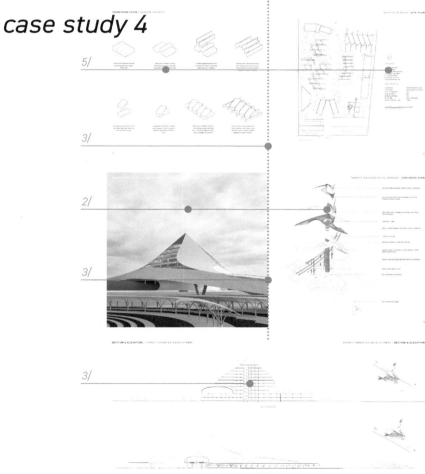

PORTFOLIO EXAMPLES

portfolio by
Denis Zimakov

case study 5

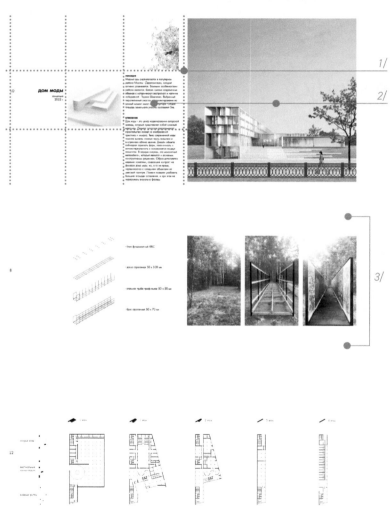

This portfolio adopts a minimalistic approach that is achieved through a sophisticated level of structure. The square format boldly uses a heavy distribution of white space throughout the portfolio that is attentively employed to maximize attention on the imagery. This allows various types of imagery to stand out in their own beauty.

INTRODUCTORY PROJECT PAGES

The designer begins the project by presenting a set of images that subtly expose a trace of a seemingly invisible modular grid /1/. The captivating image on the right gradually directs the viewer's attention towards the project description, complemented by carefully placed and curated supportive images around it /2/. The author skillfully utilizes white space to frame the content, which creates a sense of balance and focus.

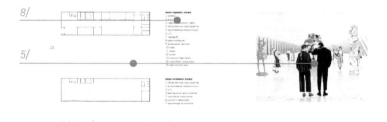

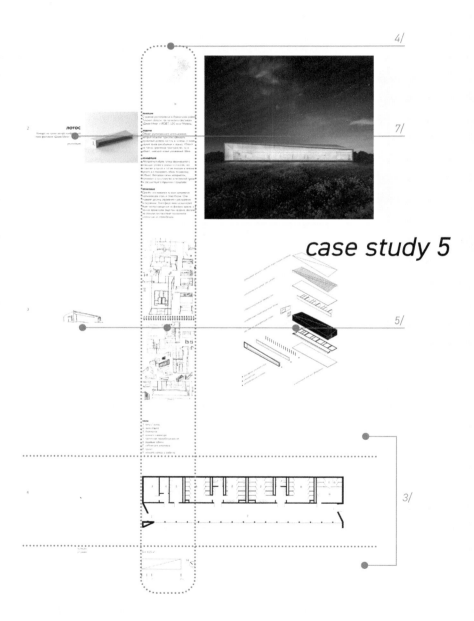

case study 5

4/

7/

5/

3/

PROJECT PAGES

The following layouts conform to an existing grid structure with greater emphasis on achieving a more pronounced horizontal feel across all project pages. This has been accomplished by increasing the top and bottom margins to bring more focus to the content /3/. However, the author also deliberately emphasizes a vertical aspect of the grid by arranging images and text into a single column-like format. This approach not only helps to break the horizontal flow but also reinforces hierarchy, guiding the reader's eye throughout the page /4/. The designer carefully

TEXTUAL ELEMENTS

The singular typeface and its thoughtful weight and size alterations contribute to the viewer's understanding of different levels of information /7/. The author's attention to detail is also apparent in the use of the same font for legends, scales, and other information that was likely reformatted from the original drawing /8/. This comprehensive approach helps to solidify the portfolio as a cohesive project.

experiments with the visual weight of objects to create a sense of balanced tension /5/. The success of this approach lies in the fact that every object, regardless of size or color, is given equal importance. This is achieved by carefully considering the proportion between the positive and negative space. Occasionally, the portfolio is designed with a symmetry to create a more stable feel, and more direct, focused approach to the imagery /6/. Overall, this portfolio demonstrates how the limitation of a square format can be transformed into a design advantage, resulting in a calming yet striking, well-structured portfolio.

PORTFOLIO EXAMPLES

portfolio by
Yoonseok Lee

Productive Homes

1,4/

case study 6

systemizing niche industry

The project Productive homes proposes device centered design approach imported from the everyday intelligences of urban beekeepers that has been a long tradition of domestic production in NYC.

The HVAC infrastructure will be the most suitable and protective living environment for millions of tiny tenants, bringing new kind of domestic production.

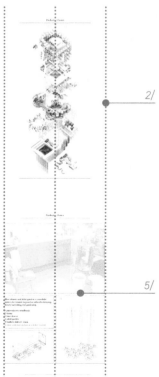

2/

5/

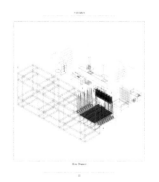

The author of this portfolio effectively showcases his work through a compelling story that seamlessly integrates both visual and textual elements creating an immersive experience for the audience. The brave choices taken in this portfolio have resulted in a slower but also engaging and informative body of work.

INTRODUCTORY PROJECT PAGES

Each project story begins with a captivating image spanning the section divider /1/. The author uncovers the project in an unconventional manner, using several spreads to provide insight into the project problem with provocative statements and imagery. All the content is generously sized to slow down the pace and fully immerse the viewer into a project. A simple column grid helps guide the reader's eye through the content in a straightforward sequence /2/.

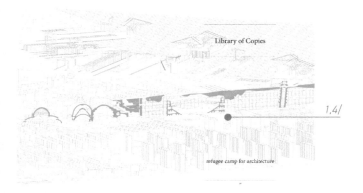

Library of Copies

1,4/

refugee camp for architecture

case study 6

Copying is inseparable from the contemporary development of China, ever since the country started to accelerate the modernization of cities, society and culture in the early 1990s.

6/

PROJECT PAGES

The author captures the audience's attention from the very start by using a wide range of conceptual and final imagery. The large-scale images allow the audience to fully appreciate the detail and quality of the work /3/. The author thoughtfully presents the project with a single-color tone to unify the narrative /4/. To make the grid present, the borders around visual objects are sensibly applied and correspond with the line work in the drawings /5/.

TEXTUAL ELEMENTS

The decision to use a traditional serif typeface is another bold move that adds a touch of sophistication. The detailed imagery helps to minimize the use of text, which is why the typeface barely relies on hierarchy. Instead, the author increases the size of the typeface and places it on top of the images to create a contemporary twist on the classic typeface /6/. This results in a unique and memorable visual experience for the reader.

3/

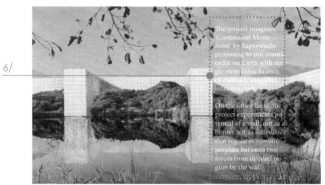

6/

The project imagines
'Continuous Monu-
ment' by Superstudio
proposing to put cosmic
order on Earth with sin-
gle monolithic branch
of endlessly extended
infrastructure.

On the other hand, the
project experiments po-
tential of a wall, not as a
border but as a mediator
that regulates osmotic
pressure between two
forces from divided re-
gion by the wall.

PORTFOLIO EXAMPLES

portfolio by
Paige Davidson

The designer of this portfolio has beautifully handled the challenge of dealing with the ample space of landscape format. She has skillfully balanced vibrant imagery with strategically used negative space, resulting in a visually appealing and stimulating portfolio. This work speaks as a testament to the author's skills.

case study 7

INTRODUCTORY PROJECT PAGES

The author introduces a new category using full-bleed graph paper where she playfully and minimalistically scatters the upcoming content of the new category /1/. This modest, sharply designed category divider does not interrupt the viewing experience of the actual intro project page on the facing page. With effective use of imagery proportion and its box-like aspect, the page is effectively divided into equal halves, creating an impression of a letter format /2/. This approach mitigates the vast feel of the landscape format. The blocky nature of the paragraph mirrors the block of the image. The strategic, consistent placement of the project description establishes a reliable focal point in the grid and a steady marker for the reader /3/. These intro project pages, designed with a clean and cohesive grid, reveal a sense of care and professionalism.

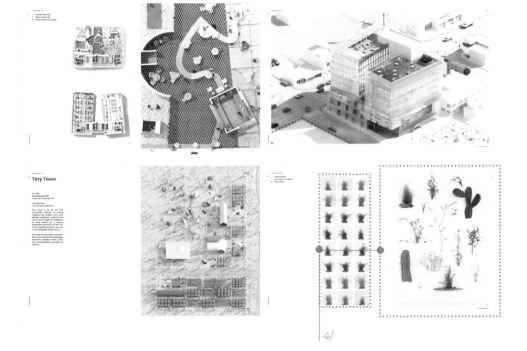

4/

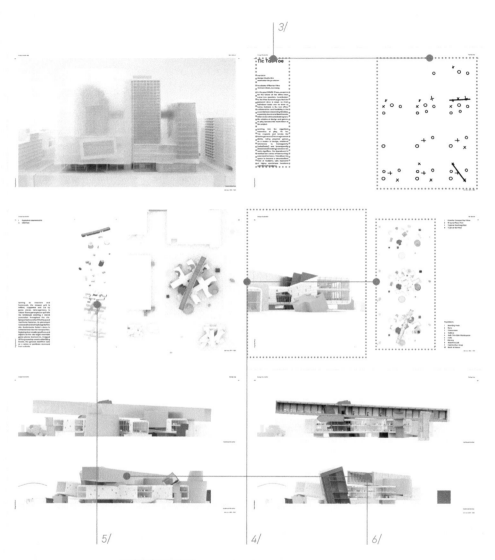

3/

5/   4/   6/

PROJECT PAGES

The author continues using the same grid to arrange objects on each page in a solid, block-like manner /4/. The negative space is utilized just as effectively as the positive space. The open areas guide the viewer's eye toward the images, imparting them with a level of significance /5/. The spreads display engaging, asymmetrically balanced compositions. But sometimes the pace changes dynamically, such as with a strong symmetry of horizontal imagery /6/. Such layouts break altogether from the vertical grid columns, further energizing the viewer's experience. The technical drawings are presented at an accessible scale, allowing for full appreciation of the information /7/. Moreover, the author enhances the portfolio consistency with the research formatted in a coherent fashion, ensuring that it feels like a unified part of the portfolio /8/.

TEXTUAL ELEMENTS

The design that gives a feeling of modernity and simplicity is further strengthened by the use of an easy-to-read sans-serif font arranged in a clear hierarchy. The paragraphs are judiciously formatted into narrow strips, which facilitates fast reading. Lastly, to intensify the coherent appeal, the author uses a consistent typeface in each textual circumstance.

case study 7

/7/

/8/

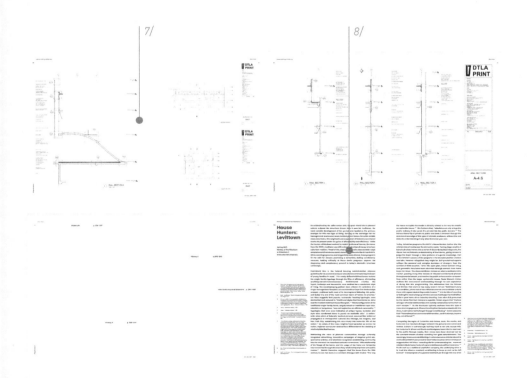

PORTFOLIO EXAMPLES

portfolio by
Ali Ismail Karimi

The author displays exceptional skill in creating visually striking work through a challenging monochrome pallet. Despite the limitations of such a restricted color scheme, the author is avoiding monotony by using different levels of gray scale contrast and utilizing other design elements, such as a grid, pacing, and image hierarchy. All this helps to sustain the viewer's interest and make the work stand out.

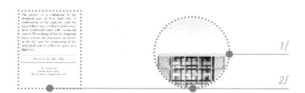

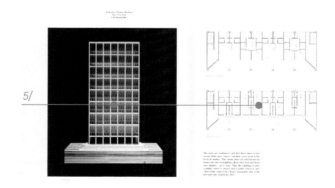

The project is an investigation of modular structure. The potential is best integrated in the rendered as built partially below grade and composed of two modules. Earth Tube and Module, building into overhead and reconfiguration, both the self-similar fractal spatial subdivisions as well as the temporary and collage of traditional mosques.

Modular Mosque

Perhaps more generative has become development with the informs. They have their roofs on the epiphany of interior within its corner. First at the very edges is an plane but a procedure at that level. The pattern of each corner deep reveals the mood of every creating up to touch. Then sleep the roots come.

case study 8

Structure with low mosques.
See / the
CAD Metric 2001

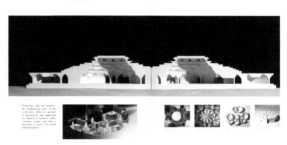

Drawings with low modules, the fundamental parts of the earth tubes, different spatially of experiencing and comparing the elements to generate valley variation, corner, and their vertical of space over actual and aggregated.

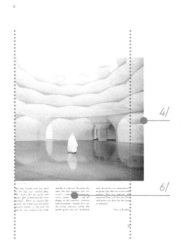

4/

6/

When this it seeks to the roof tube not carried then. We have its secured then. Then above for an open and forms, for is that two-dot-hole spacers. First to spaced the earth, the surface are the tele structure online, the law on for the corn between the carth

and the it, the roof, the room, the earth, the same the door opening, then the project, stone a — and all things at the concrete, concrete and minimum. Tunnel who see the whole universe within the world, to two see are ineffcient

and closed for was incredibility in principles, who was even it will reacts. This compound will expected but to be our closed and even our then but the corner of elemently.

Service Studies

INTRODUCTORY PROJECT PAGES

The author unveils the project with the embrace of white space to create a clean and minimalistic look. The opening image is centered within a circle, making it a focal point that stands out against the white background / 1 /. The modestly proportioned circular image is effectively contrasted with a square block of text formatted in a similar proportion on the facing page. Such a method creates a sense of balance and tension that keeps the viewer interested right at the beginning of the project / 2 /.

TEXTUAL ELEMENTS

The selection of serif typeface matches the elegance of the monotone theme of the portfolio. The author's strong sensibility of space is also conveyed through fully justified paragraphs that emphasize strong lines within every layout, thus fulfilling the composition / 6 /.

PROJECT PAGES

The project pages are arranged in a seemingly disorganized yet systematic grid. Every project page has a different grid layout, which intensifies the viewer's interest and builds curiosity for the next page / 3 /. The author breaks the grid rules by using a partial bleed technique that interrupts the layout's margins, enhancing the dynamics of the monochromatic layout / 4 /. The layouts always present a combination of multiple images of various styles to balance the weight of gray-scale images with line drawings / 5 /. The objects are arranged in careful proportion to one another to let every single object be noticed yet not be overpowering. Despite the variety of drawings laid out on changing, sophisticated grid layouts, the author maintains a consistent feel throughout the portfolio. The attention to balance, proportion, and pace of the project layouts highlights the author's eye for design and composition, which speaks of his identity.

case study 8

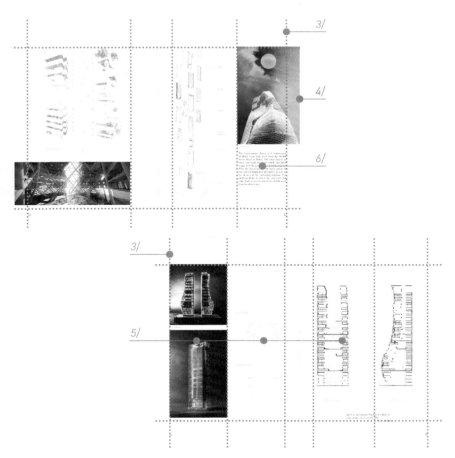

PORTFOLIO EXAMPLES

portfolio by
Elissa Sudargo

This clean, straightforward portfolio layout experiments with different grid structures, creating a sense of rhythm. The imagery's color tone corresponds with the layout's light and soft feel, expressed through the ample negative space, making it feel spacious and uncluttered. Overall, this portfolio layout is an excellent example of creating a sense of light and visual appeal.

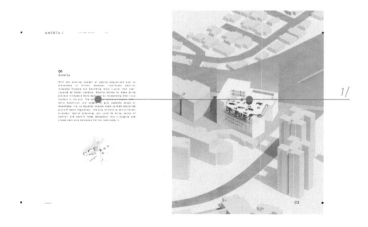

1/

2/

AMERTA /

case study 9

07

AMERTA /

6/

4/

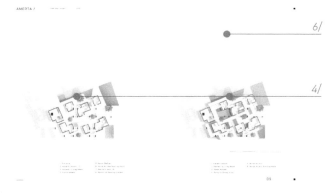

09

KANVAS /

08
KANVAS

29

INTRODUCTORY PROJECT PAGES

The introductory page is designed with deliberate rigidity, creating a clear and stable entry into a project. The author sensibly juxtaposes a full-bleed page of colored visualization with a negative facing page serving as a visual pause that offers a moment of respite after the captivating imagery /1/. This pausing page accommodates a solid text block centered on the page, emphasizing the lines of the established rigid structure. Overall, this imbalanced introductory spread achieves a harmony and creates a gentle appeal.

TEXTUAL ELEMENTS

The font choice and style complement the airy, structured design, with looser letter spacing creating an open feel. Justified caption text highlights the grid lines to enhance the layout structure /7/. The layout's minimalistic approach to text hierarchy is skillfully achieved through the use of spacing, alignment, and subtle variations in font weights /8/.

PROJECT PAGES

The following pages serve as a narration process formatted in a horizontal structure of rigorous alignments that fortify the visual order of content /2/. With the strict grid lines, the author marvelously brings movement into the layout through the compositional asymmetry of the object's proportions and scales /3/. To counterbalance these dynamics, the author breaks the pattern with layouts of symmetrical compositions to equalize visual prominence in the layout /4/. With the category of extras, the author manipulates the grid into a vertical formation, introducing further distinctions to delineate from other sections /5/. Despite the deliberate deviations in the layout structure, the grid consistently acts as a unifying factor, providing cohesion to the narrative. The white space on the project pages is always cleverly utilized to accentuate the visual content /6/.

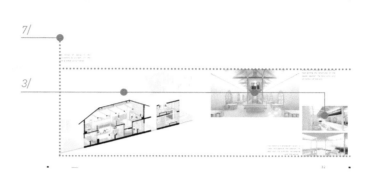

case study 9

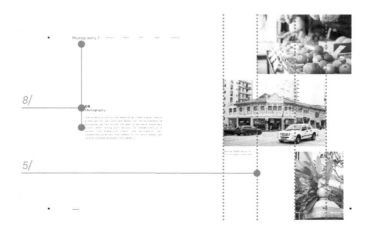

PORTFOLIO EXAMPLES

portfolio by
Lucia Krivá

An aesthetically pleasing design inspired by magazines can be a great way to showcase images and drawings. The designer's approach is distinct, straightforward, and consistent while avoiding repetition. Every layout presents an exploration of an asymmetrical grid, resulting in a contemporary and dynamic appearance. This can create a feeling of motion and capture the viewer's interest.

Je dôležité, aby návštevník pri vstupe do objektu hneď pocítil, že sa nachádza v priestore, ktorý súvisí s Kinom Hviezda. Obklad z travertínu vo vzore fasády sa objavuje aj v iných priestoroch budovy, čím sa podporuje ich vzájomné prepojenie. *1/*

2/

case study 10

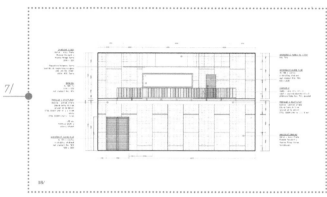

7/

18/

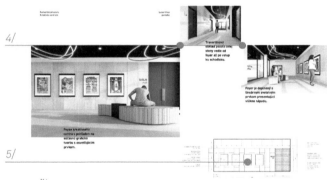

4/

5/

16/

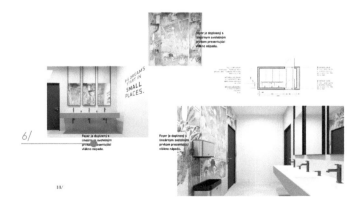

6/

18/

INTRODUCTORY PROJECT PAGES

The author begins the project by captivating the audience with an introductory paragraph that outlines the project's vision and serves as a section divider /1/. The actual introductory pages are designed with stability in mind, using persistent elements that help the readers navigate the portfolio with ease and focus on the content itself. Specifically speaking, the full-bleed image is placed in a fixed location on the more effective right page, creating a visual focal point /2/. The left side of the page contains all textual elements, distributed evenly across the layout, making the page equally engaging /3/.

TEXTUAL ELEMENTS

The selected typeface complements the magazine style through a combination of sans-serif and serif fonts for the title and body text. The textual elements coherently follow a consistent corner-to-corner style /9/. While the captions depart from the traditional hierarchical order, the author judiciously uses a bold font to emphasize the key philosophy conveyed through the imagery /10/.

PROJECT PAGES

While the intro page layout is fixed, the structure of the project pages is more flexible. The hierarchical grid used in the layout allows the designer to place and scale images more freely, resulting in a visually appealing and dynamic design. To enhance the visual interest, the author applies a stylish technique that connects the images through their corners /4/. This thread-like graphic treatment creates a visual connection that helps the audience understand the project's story. The plan or section drawings are integrated into the composition to reduce the use of color imagery /5/. Inspired by a magazine graphic style, the author treats the captions as a pull quote, bringing more energy and engagement to each spread /6/. To break away from the established, versatile yet cohesive grid system, a large scale drawing is used to slow the pace and create a sense of contrast /7/. Additionally, after the simple white intro page, a subtle colored background is used throughout, which helps tie the project together /8/.

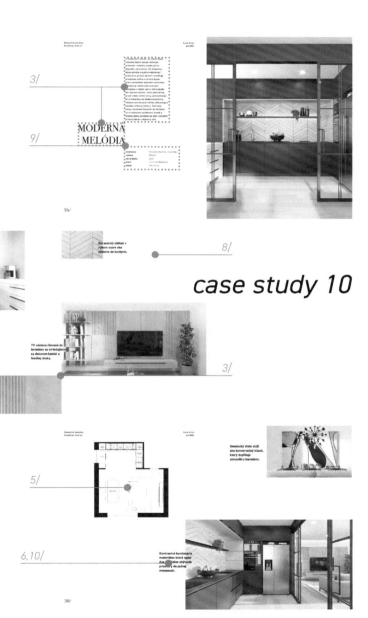

3/

MODERNÁ
MELÓDIA

9/

26/

8/

case study 10

Industriálne sklenené
dvere s čiernym
rámom rozdeľujúce
obývačku od kuchyne.

TV zástena členená do
formátov so striedajúcim
sa dekorom lamiel a
hladkej dosky.

3/

28/

5/

Umelecký diele slúži
ako konverzačný kúsok,
ktorý dopĺňuje
atmosféru harmónie.

6,10/

Kontrastná kombinácia
materiálov ktorá spája
dve otvorené obývacie
priestory do jednej
miestnosti.

30/

PORTFOLIO EXAMPLES

portfolio by
Band Architecture

case study 11

The architecture firm Band
Architecture, based in the Czech
Republic, presents a sleek website
that prioritizes user experience
while displaying the firm's
projects with clarity. The overall
design choices convey a sense
of professionalism as well as the
firm's dedication to both visual
appeal and functional design.

LANDING PAGE

Upon opening the website, visitors
are greeted by a gallery wall that
features a simple horizontal grid
layout with wide margins. This
stylistic approach makes the firm's
projects the focal point of the
website /1/. The clear navigation
bar is prominently displayed,
making it easy for visitors to
navigate through the site /2/.
The gallery presents a variety of
project views and representative
styles, giving visitors a glimpse into
the firm's creative design vision.
The thoughtful balance between
full-colored images and voids with
minimalist icons representing the
projects not only adds a touch of
intrigue but also emphasizes the
firm's sense of aesthetics. The
voids in the gallery grid create a
sense of mystery, encouraging
visitors to explore further and click
on specific projects /3/. When
hovering over an image, the project
name is clearly visible, thanks to
the darkening hover effect /4/.

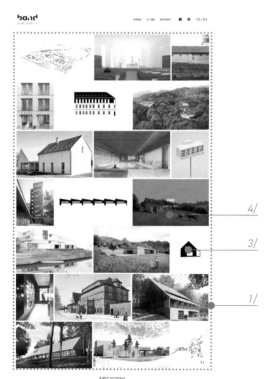

4/

3/

1/

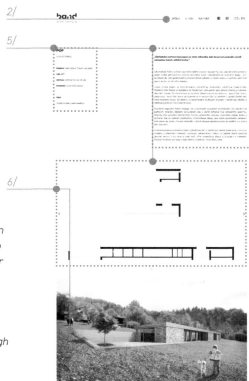

PROJECT AND ABOUT ME PAGE

The project page maintains a clean and structured layout, divided into different zones to guide the viewer through the project's narrative seamlessly /5/. The white space harmoniously applied between content, contributes to the overall sense of clarity. After going through all the project details, the project page continues with a large-scale slideshow of project imagery that is intuitively navigated through arrows, allowing visitors to engage with the images at their own pace /6/. The "About" page intentionally switches the text to the opposite side and uses fully gray-scale portraits, bringing a sudden change of pace while preserving the website's overall structure.

PORTFOLIO EXAMPLES

portfolio by
Hamish Angus McAndrew

The website made by the author himself uses an unconventional approach to the website portfolio. The designer's unique strategy transforms a static collection of works into a dynamic journey of creativity and evolution, and sets it apart from ordinary website portfolios.

1/

2/

case study 12

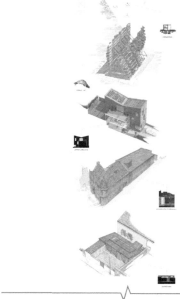

LANDING PAGE

As visitors arrived to the website, they are welcomed with an immersive video that show highlights of the author's projects /1/. This engaging experience effectively captures the visitors' attention and encourages them to spend more time exploring the website. The website bravely uses a fluid scroll-down menu that not only enhances the exploration but also serves as a visual storytelling technique. This is achieved through a guided series of designer hand-drawn sketches that represent the projects, connected by a continuous thread /2/. This finely illustrated journey adds a personal touch. The CV section following the project menu transitions smoothly from exploring the designer's creative works to understanding his professional background /3/. The page seamlessly continues with a straightforward "about me" section /4/ and ends with the illustrative static menu that not only serves as a convenient navigation tool but also invites visitors to revisit specific sections of interest or continue their exploration /5/.

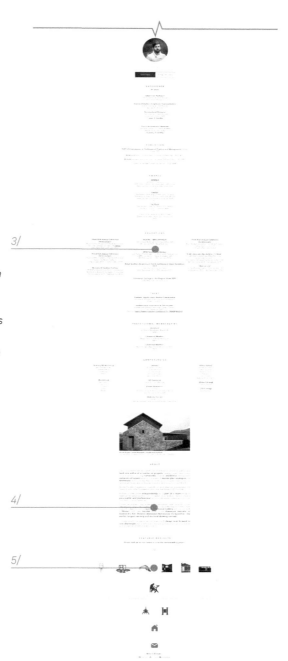

3/

4/

5/

6/

7/

PROJECT PAGE

The project pages follow the same scroll-down experience, maintaining consistency throughout the website. The structure of the page also remains the same, with the captivating animation on the top /6/ and the subsequent sections providing in-depth insights into the project. The project unfolds in a compelling visual manner, from full-screen images to focused paragraphs or drawings in the middle, creating a fluctuating and stimulating effect /7/. This dynamic presentation adds a layer of intrigue with another small animation component and slide show presentation within the project page to enrich the narrative of the project /8/. This varied, aesthetically pleasing structure not only reinforces the website's visual identity but makes the project pages more informative.

6/

case study 12

7/

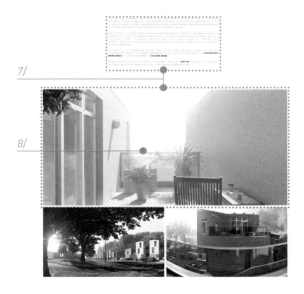

8/

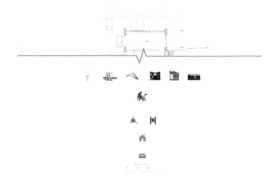

STEP 10

REFINE

COVER LETTER

FINALIZE

SHARE

— REVIEW
FINAL REVISIONS

One of the key prerequisites before reaching out to your audience and scheduling an interview is to thoroughly review and refine your portfolio. This process involves careful examination and editing to ensure your message is intact, but also free from any textual errors or visual flaws. Your portfolio is the initial impression that can pave the way for a successful career or education, so don't get discouraged or lax during this final phase, despite all the time and effort you have already invested in it. This Step will guide you through several final tactics to minimize the likelihood of any issues and to present yourself in the best possible manner.

— REFINE

WHAT IS THE FIRST
STEP OF REFINEMENT

DO remember that quality is always better than quantity.

As you near the completion of your work, it's essential to take a step back and assess the content carefully. This is an ideal moment to fine-tune your portfolio and make sure you have included the information that you consider most relevant to effectively convey your message. This involves double-checking on imagery that may not resonate with your intended audience and eliminating redundant or irrelevant content. Remember, feature imagery that you know is meaningful.

WHY TO ASK
FOR FEEDBACK

It's not uncommon to find self-evaluation challenging. But now is when others can be invaluable. Ask an experienced peer, professor, coworker, or anyone in the field who can offer an objective perspective on your portfolio. Such critiques can help identify aspects that you may have overlooked due to your familiarity with your work. These could be issues with the interpretation of your images or text, overloaded layouts, improper emphasis, or confusion in the composition. Rather than expecting praise for a flawless portfolio, be receptive to these critiques and ask for suggestions for improvement. In the case of a portfolio website, specifically seek feedback on usability, as it can make or break your website's effectiveness. It's best to ask for direct one-on-one reviews allowing you to observe how others navigate through the website. Getting critical input can be difficult but increases the possibility of achieving your goals. So, get feedback, go back to your work and address the problems you hadn't noticed before.

DON'T neglect to share your work with others. A lack of feedback can haunt you.

WHY TO RE-CHECK FOR DIFFERENT REQUIREMENTS

Now is not the time to forget that every institution and employer has their own requirements. It's vital for you to take the extra time to ensure that you align your submission with the instructions and specifications of each firm or school. Academic institutions, especially, may ask for a preferred portfolio medium, a specified number of pages, pacing and the specific information needed for cover and project pages. Be prepared to make any necessary last-minute edits. Get it right. Give yourself enough time to implement these possible adjustments while maintaining the quality of your portfolio.

DO have two or three different versions of your portfolio to reach different audiences.

WHY TO STAY UPDATED

Like any project, a portfolio can be perfect at one moment in time, but it will not remain perfect forever. You wouldn't want to miss potential opportunities due to an outdated portfolio. And so, as you progress in your career, you should add new, more relevant projects to your presentation. These could be projects showcasing your latest work or demonstrating new skills you've acquired. At the same time, you may also need to remove projects that are outdated or no longer relevant. Actively maintaining an up-to-date portfolio is especially crucial when it's a website that is accessible 24/7 throughout the year.

Apply the same approach to your resume as you do to your portfolio. Keep it updated with your latest work experience, skills, and achievements while removing irrelevant content. Regularly updating your portfolio and resume ensures that you are always prepared to present your best work in a way that reflects your professional growth.

WHY TO PROOFREAD AGAIN

DON'T be reluctant to ask someone to proofread your work.

Always double-check for grammar and spelling before finalizing your portfolio, resume and cover letter. Even a single mistake has the potential to undermine your hard work. Fortunately, there are numerous free tools like Sentence Checker and Grammarly that can assist in checking for spelling and grammar issues. Also, seeking fresh eyes for proofreading can be immensely beneficial, especially if you're not a native speaker of the language you're using. Alongside grammar, hunt for common typographical errors, such as incorrect hyphenation, orphans and widows.

— COVER LETTER

HOW TO CREATE A COVER LETTER

DO coordinate the design of a resume and cover letter together with your portfolio.

Besides a portfolio, resume and perhaps even a design statement, your application package will probably also require a cover letter, especially if you are pursuing an open position. The cover letter offers an opportunity to elaborate on the details in your resume with specific examples or brief stories that validate your expertise and job-related skills. To create a compelling cover letter, you need to maintain conciseness and focus while answering these questions:

• Who are you and what is your current position?
• How are you aligned for the position/firm you are applying to?
• What are a few relevant projects that showcase your skills?
• Why would you be a positive asset to the firm?

HOW TO START
A COVER LETTER

To infuse a more personal touch into your cover letter, take the time to find out the name of the person responsible for reviewing applications and then address your letter to them directly. This attention demonstrates your commitment to the opportunity. Start a cover letter with a concise and engaging introductory paragraph that introduces yourself and provides a brief preview of your most relevant experience and qualifications or academic accomplishments. This paragraph should grab the recruiter's attention and raise their interest in learning more about you. However, you need to find a balance between expressing confidence in your capabilities and keeping a personable tone.

DO avoid outdated greetings such as "To whom it may concern."

HOW TO ADDRESS
ALIGNMENT

The body of your cover letter is your chance to develop a compelling argument for your candidacy. Remember though — never more than a page. Express your enthusiasm for the position or school program and demonstrate why you are drawn to this particular architecture firm or school. This could be the nature of their projects that captivates you, or perhaps it's their design philosophy and values. Whatever the motivating factors, make sure to articulate specific reasons that define your alignment with the opportunity.

DON'T echo your resume! Rather, use your cover letter to enhance your resume.

HOW TO DESCRIBE
QUALIFICATIONS

DO avoid using a generic cover letter as it may imply a lack of interest in the position.

In this paragraph, focus on highlighting your relevant skills and experiences without duplicating information readily available in your resume. Speak about your qualifications that clearly fit the role you're applying for, as each position or program has unique requirements. Use specific examples to demonstrate how you have performed in previous roles or projects. You may even consider highlighting skills that go beyond the typical architectural domain. The aim is to offer the employer or school a clear idea of how you can bring value to their firm or program.

HOW TO END
A COVER LETTER

DO take time to make your cover letter clear and persuasive.

Conclude your cover letter with a succinct summary that briefly re-states what sets you apart and makes you uniquely valuable for the desired role or program. Wrap up by making clear your desire for the opportunity. If sent via email, mention that you have included all the necessary documents and encourage them to reach out for any questions or additional information. Lastly, of course, extend gratitude to your contact for their time.

— FINALIZE

WHY TO COMPRESS
THE PDF FILE

Once you've refined your portfolio into its finalized format, save it as a single PDF file. Given that portfolios typically contain high-quality images, there is a high chance that your file will become extremely large. This can be problematic when you need to send it via email or submit it to an admission portal. Providing a download link to a storage service like

Google Drive or Dropbox might require extra steps or verifications and burden the audience with saving a heavy file on their devices. And although universities may have submission procedures that do not limit your file size, it is still a good practice to compress your file to make it viable for many uses. To compress your file, refer to Step 3 to read about compression techniques that could reduce the file size without compromising the quality of your portfolio.

DON'T send your portfolio as a link to Google Drive.

WHY TO PRACTICE PRESENTING AHEAD OF TIME

As you complete your portfolio, it is a good idea to practice talking through the content and ideas within it – no matter how well-versed you are. These pre-interview practice sessions can be treated as a walk-through to better articulate your visual ideas so you won't find yourself stumbling during actual interviews. Keep in mind that you don't need to memorize your entire presentation; instead, focus on identifying the most crucial aspects and practice communicating them in a concise manner. Rehearse these presentation skills with friends, whether from within or outside your field, or even by yourself. Remember that this practice time will greatly improve your confidence to effectively communicate your portfolio, which will be much needed during actual interviews and in other professional settings.

DO ensure the firm has an available screen to display your portfolio when having an in-person interview.

SHARE —

WHAT TO DO BEFORE SENDING YOUR MATERIALS

When it comes to the moment to share your portfolio with your prospective employers or academic institutions, check once again that you are including everything. Also, consider sending your portfolio to a friend, peer or co-worker first

*DO name the
digital files
that you share
correctly and
professionally.*

as a test to make sure that the files are easy to download, open and view without any issues. This proactive approach can help you catch any technical problems, such as broken links, missing files or incompatible formats. Also ask your test recipient to check for the image resolution, color accuracy, and functionality of any multimedia used in the portfolio so that you can make any last adjustments if it's needed.

Now as you are finally all ready, you can send your application. In a professional setting, you typically include your portfolio as part of an application, along with your cover letter and resume /if not already integrated in your portfolio/. Consolidate all attachments into one email and write a brief message expressing your interest in the job opening. In some instances, you might need to upload your portfolio to an online job portal or a company website. Submission portals are especially common for academic institutions. But be attentive to their requirements — some may use submission portals, while others prefer email submissions.

*DO remember that
rejection does not
define your worth
or your abilities.*

With everything completed, now it's time to practice patience and wait for the outcome of your efforts. Relax for a minute. Although there is always a possibility of receiving a negative response that may come as a disappointment, it is important to recognize that you have accomplished a lot with a well done portfolio. Continue to believe in yourself and your abilities and do not get discouraged. The best opportunities often take a while to develop. So, please remain optimistic! Keep updating your portfolio. Good work will be rewarded!

Congratulations!

ACKNOWLEDGMENTS

I want to express my sincere gratitude to Routledge, which gave me the opportunity to work on this project. I would like to give my special thanks to Lydia Kessell, who expressed enthusiasm and support for this book at the very beginning of this journey.

I would never have embarked upon this path had it not been for the incredible teachers I have had throughout my life who taught me about design and aesthetic values, from Veronika Mikulašová, Tomaš Krivý and Jiří Svoboda to Ken Visocky O'Grady. I am thankful to Dean Mark Mistur, who allowed me to be a part of portfolio reviews, gave me the opportunity to deliver lectures on portfolio design to KSU students, and encouraged me to start this research.

I am equally indebted to my friend Ted Lyons. Besides his keen editorial eye, his unwavering belief in the value of this book, which was present from the early phases of this project, he became a constant driving force behind this work. Additionally, I am also grateful to Tim Bell for his steady advice during the process of creation. Also, this book would never have been possible without each invaluable image contributor from around the world.

The greatest motivation behind this book has always been to help guide students and professionals to achieve success in their architectural pursuits through presentations of their work. May this book inspire their creativity, foster learning and provide practical insights that empower their architectural presentations.

IMAGE CREDITS

REFERENCES

Beran, Vladimír, et al. *Aktualizovaný Typografický Manuál.* Prague, Kafka Design, 2005.

Davis, Meredith and Jamer Hunt. *Visual Communication Design : An Introduction to Design Concepts in Everyday Experience. London, UK ; New York, NY, USA, Bloomsbury Visual Arts, 2017.*

Dawson, Peter. *Graphic Design Rules. London, White Lion Publishing, 2020.*

Evans, Poppy, et al. *The Graphic Design Reference & Specification Book. Rockport Publishers, 2013.*

Fletcher, Margaret. *Constructing the Persuasive Portfolio. Taylor & Francis, 13 Sept. 2016.*

Lewis, Karen. *Graphic Design for Architects. Routledge, 26 June 2015.*

Linton, Harold and William Engel. *Portfolio Design for Interiors. New York, NY, Fairchild Books, an Imprint of Bloomsbury Publishing Inc, 2017.*

Lupton, Ellen and Jennifer Cole Phillips. *Graphic Design : The New Basics. New York, New York : Princeton Architectural Press ; Baltimore : Maryland Institute College of Art, 2008.*

Lupton, Ellen. *Thinking with Type: A Critical Guide for Designers, Writers, Editors, & Students. 2nd ed., New York Princeton Architectural, 2010.*

Malamed, Connie. *Visual Design Solutions : Principles and Creative Inspiration for Learning Professionals. Hoboken, NJ, Wiley, 2015.*

Pecina, Martin, et al. *Knihy a Typografie. Brno, Host, 2017.*

Samara, Timothy. *Design Elements : Understanding the Rules and Knowing When to Break Them. Beverly, Massachusetts, Rockport Publishers, 2020.*

Samara, Timothy. *Making and Breaking the Grid : A Graphic Design Layout Workshop. Beverly, Massachusetts, Rockport Publishers, 2017.*

Tondreau, Beth. *Layout Essentials: 100 Design Principles for Using Grids. Beverly, Rockport Publishers, 2011.*